# OPPORTUNITIES

## DATE DUE

| | | | |
|---|---|---|---|
| | | | |
| | | | |
| | | | |
| | | | |
| | | | |
| | | | |
| | | | |
| | | | |
| | | | |
| | | | |
| | | | |
| | | | |
| | | | |
| | | | |
| | | | |

D1470243

# OPPORTUNITIES

## in

# Eye Care Careers

### REVISED EDITION

**KATHLEEN BELIKOFF**

## *VGM Career Books*

*Chicago   New York   San Francisco   Lisbon   London   Madrid   Mexico City*
*Milan   New Delhi   San Juan   Seoul   Singapore   Sydney   Toronto*

[MAY 1 6 2008]

*The McGraw-Hill Companies*

Library of Congress Cataloging-in-Publication Data

Opportunities in eye care careers / Kathleen Belikoff. — Rev. ed.
  p.    cm. — (VGM opportunities series)
  ISBN 0-07-141150-X
  1. Ophthalmology—Vocational guidance.    2. Optometry—Vocational
guidance.    3. Opticianry—Vocational guidance.    4. Ophthalmic assistants—
Vocational guidance.    I. Title.    II. Series.

RE72.A37    2004
616.7'023—dc21                                            2003049731

1 2 3 4 5 6 7 8 9 0    LBM/LBM    2 1 0 9 8 7 6 5 4 3

ISBN 0-07-141150-X

Interior design by Rattray Design

McGraw-Hill books are available at special quantity discounts to use as premiums and
sales promotions, or for use in corporate training programs. For more information,
please write to the Director of Special Sales, Professional Publishing, McGraw-Hill, Two
Penn Plaza, New York, NY 10121-2298. Or contact your local bookstore.

This book is printed on acid-free paper.

In memory of I. Donald Snook, Jr.
1939–2002
Leader, Teacher, Writer, Mentor, and Friend

# Contents

Volunteer work. Part-time jobs. Internships. Find
a mentor. Virtual eye care careers: surfing the
Internet.

The eye. How we see. Maintaining visual health.
Normal aging. Especially for women. Disorders of
the visual system. Diseases of the visual system.

# Foreword

As a physician, researcher, and teacher, I have had the opportunity to discuss eye care careers with many young men and women. When asked for my advice on their suitability for this career choice, I tell them that the successful ophthalmologists I know have high ideals and realistic goals. These derive from the exhilarating gratification of personally improving the quality of life for many people and from the humbling knowledge that this wonderful contribution to humankind is possible only by pursuing a rigorous, never-ending course of study and by constantly finding fault with the current state of patient care. Research is part of the process of constant improvement. This is one reason why people choose eye care as a career. It is a daily challenge with short-term and long-term rewards.

Because the world is changing at such a rapid rate, I am often asked if someone can select an occupation in health care that will not become obsolete before it is time to retire. Personally, I have found that the best strategy for coping with the uncertainty of the future is to stay well informed about one's chosen field, so that one can identify and act on the best career opportunities. For the reader who would like to make an informed decision about choosing a career in ophthalmology, optometry, opticianry, or a related field, *Opportunities in Eye Care Careers* is a good starting place. Ms. Belikoff has presented an accurate overview of the eye care professions and offers resources for more information if needed. I hope that readers of this book will heed this advice and try an eye care career on for size.

Stuart L. Fine, M.D.
Professor and Chair
Department of Ophthalmology
Director, Scheie Eye Institute
University of Pennsylvania Health System

# Preface

Almost every day there are advances in the diagnosis and treatment of eye diseases. It is not surprising that the researchers who discover new eye care technologies, as well as the people who provide everyday vision care, are among the most respected and trusted people in the health care industry and in our society.

The purpose of this book is to help the reader make an informed decision about whether his or her career goals match the opportunities available in the eye care field. Making a decision about a future in eye care should include three goals:

1. Gaining a realistic perspective and understanding of today's ophthalmic industry and the requirements, expectations, and roles of its present workforce
2. Speculating on how you might fit into the future employment scenario

3. Comparing your goals, philosophy, and personality with those of other people who have found satisfaction in this field of work

Of these, the third goal is the one that is the hardest to achieve. It involves more than reading. It entails doing some soul-searching about what you really expect from your work and being honest about what you, as a person, can bring to the marketplace. It helps to go out and talk to the people who are in the job that you think you want. Although they are busy people, they were once in your shoes. Usually, they are glad to reminisce about their experiences and give you some valuable advice about what they would do differently. There are some other ideas in Chapter 9, Trying an Eye Care Career on for Size, to think about before you take the plunge. One that you might find intriguing is the advice on virtual career experiences that you can acquire by "surfing" the World Wide Web.

Most of this book focuses on the first goal. The first chapter is an introduction to what is happening in eye care today. You will see that it is a very diverse and dynamic field with many career opportunities. The second chapter will give you some historical perspective on the ancient world of eye care and a whimsical look into the crystal ball of the future that could be the world in which you work. All of this will prepare you for the middle portion of the book, which provides detailed information about particular job categories. The final part of the book offers "consumer information" about eye and vision care, and there are resource guides in the appendixes to help you find more information about these occupations and to prepare for career training.

Somewhere in the process of trying this career on for size, you may come to the conclusion that it is not for you. If this is the case, then reading this book will have helped you in other ways. Even though you will never be an ophthalmologist, you will know when to see one and what to expect of him or her. Even though you may never discover a cure for glaucoma, you will know what it is and how to use the proper terminology in discussing eye-related problems with your doctor. Even though you may never rehabilitate a blind person, you will know what to do when you meet someone who is visually impaired on the street. And although you will not make your living from eye care, perhaps you will donate your old glasses, some money, or some time to an organization that provides services to the visually impaired. In some way, you will use what you learn to improve the quality of eye care for yourself, your family, or those around you.

# 1

# Today's Opportunities in Eye Care Careers

Your first impression of your eye doctor may have caused you to read this book. If you had a good experience and think you would like to follow in his or her footsteps, learning everything you can about the eye care field is a good start. Or perhaps you're one of the many people who is confused about what kind of doctor you would see for a serious eye injury and where you would find this person. Having a good understanding of the complex system of people, places, and services that comprise the eye care delivery system may help you make a good career choice. It also will allow you to make informed decisions about your own health care. The purpose of this chapter is to give you some general information about the distinctions among eye care professionals—ophthalmologists, optometrists, and opticians—as well as to describe several other eye care careers that might be new to you.

As in other areas of health care and in other professions, the distinction among the roles of eye care providers is constantly changing, and the boundaries between professions are sometimes blurred. This is what makes eye care a career with so many opportunities.

## What Is Eye Care?

According to the American Association of Ophthalmology, eye care is defined as: ". . . services provided by or under the direction of a qualified eye or health professional for the prevention, diagnosis, or treatment of refractive error, disease, injury, or disability affecting the eye, adnexal [surrounding] structures, visual system, or related systems."

There are many different types of eye care workers who have to master a wide range of very technical skills to treat not just the eye, but other parts of the body that have to do with sight. This is not a career for just anyone! It requires an initial investment in educational preparation and training, the ability to keep up with rapid changes in technology, effective "people skills," and the business acumen to survive in a competitive marketplace.

Perfect eyesight, like many other aspects of good health, is something that most people take for granted—until they lose it. It is hard to believe that in a society that is so technologically advanced, half of the population of the United States currently needs some sort of vision care. Ninety-six percent of those over the age of sixty-five have vision problems, and only half can afford appropriate care. Vision is not only something that is necessary to perform activities of daily living; it is essential to the enjoyment of all of the special things in life. Of all the senses—including hearing, smell, touch, and taste—sight is the most highly developed in physically healthy human beings and is considered by many to be the most precious. Here are a few examples of how vision—and the professionals who care for it—contribute to our enjoyment of everyday life.

## Learning

We are never too old to stop learning. Even when our formal schooling ends, we must constantly acquire new knowledge, skills, and aptitudes to deal with new situations. Eighty-five percent of all learning is acquired through vision. In fact, visual learning is so important that it requires one-third of the brain to handle the images that we must process. A learning exercise such as reading involves not only being able to see printed characters accurately, but also the ability to understand the symbols on which the eye focuses. The use of audiovisual media and microcomputers has put additional emphasis on the student's ability to process complex images and has emphasized the need to help those with learning disorders such as dyslexia. Vision specialists are an important part of the treatment team of special education teachers, psychologists, family members, and peers, and they play an active role in the successful therapy for children and adults with learning disorders.

## Driving

Historians characterized the twentieth century as the "transportation age." Today, almost every family has a car, and those who do not are users of public transportation. Every driver must pass a vision test before receiving a license. Vision experts design these evaluations, and examiners are trained to administer the tests. Of particular concern to everyone is the number of aging drivers still on the highways. Sunbelt states, which attract a large population of retired persons, have special requirements for older drivers. Some of the popular programs at senior centers are speakers from eye care professional associations who address issues related to vision testing and its importance in driving defensively and maintaining good driving skills.

## Working

Occupational eye care is a growing area of interest among workers, employers, and insurers. It is also highly regulated by the Occupational Safety and Health Act. The Prevention Blindness America program estimates that there are more than a thousand eye injuries on each working day. Aside from the obvious concern for the protection of workers' vision, there are studies that show that the cost of poor vision is staggering to the U.S. economy. Researchers estimate that nearly one-third of all "spoiled work" is caused by poor vision, costing industry billions of dollars each year.

## Recreation and Sports

Leisure time in America is increasing, and people are expecting eye care that will improve their performance and enjoyment of recreational activities as well as prevent eye injuries while at play. An early study of Olympic athletes showed that nearly 35 percent needed corrective lenses. Protective eyewear is required or recommended by many professional athletic associations in sports such as marksmanship and racquetball. Many athletes, both professionals and weekend amateurs, wear specially designed eyewear; there are even corrective goggles for underwater sports. The popularity of video and computer games has generated concern among eye professionals about eyestrain, especially among children. (Chapter 10 provides guidelines for safe play.)

## *Enjoying Other People*

Perhaps the most important facet of vision is its effect on interpersonal relationships. There are many colloquial expressions that refer to the importance the eyes play in body language. For instance, someone who seems untrustworthy may be described as having "shifty eyes." A popular psychologist recently advised women that men make up their minds about potential mates within seven seconds of seeing a female for the first time. Perhaps this need to make a good first impression explains the explosive new market for tinted contact lenses, fashion frames, and oculoplastic surgery to improve the appearance of the eye area. LASIK (Laser Assisted in Keratomileusis), an elective laser surgery that eliminates the need to wear corrective lenses, also is becoming more popular for cosmetic reasons. Both women and men are taking advantage of these advances in eye care, providing professionals in the field with rewarding and challenging career opportunities.

# Meet the Eye Care Team

Almost everyone at one time or another has had a vision test. Eye care begins when the obstetrician checks the eye movements of a newborn baby. Most people's recollection of their first experience with eye care is when the school nurse examined their eyes on the first day of kindergarten. Or maybe it was in their teens when a driver's license examiner asked them to read an eye chart. For the many youngsters who wear glasses, an ophthalmologist, optometrist, or optician was the person who helped them read better or made it possible for them to hit a baseball.

People who work in eye care have many different levels of education and on-the-job experience. State licensing boards and professional certification organizations also require many eye care workers to meet certain standards of practice and determine the types of care that they are allowed to provide. This is called *scope of practice*. The professionals described below summarize the scope of practice for the major eye care careers.

There are basically three types of eye care workers. Professionals are the people we most often refer to as *doctors*. Technicians and technologists are the *professional extenders* who perform certain vital support services. And then there are some interesting related occupations that require professional training outside the visual sciences.

## Professionals

There are three major categories of professionals:

### Ophthalmologists

Ophthalmologists are doctors of medicine or osteopathy who have received training beyond medical school in the specialty of eye care and diseases. They are the only professionals who are licensed to diagnose and treat all eye problems and provide total care.

### Optometrists

Optometrists complete four years of graduate education at a college of optometry to receive the degree of Doctor of Optometry (O.D.). They are qualified to examine patients for eye problems and to prescribe and fit eyeglasses and contact lenses. In many states and several provinces, optometrists may prescribe and administer drugs in the diagnosis and treatment of eye diseases.

### Opticians

Opticians can fit and dispense glasses and contact lenses based on prescriptions written by other professionals. Their training varies among states and ranges from on-the-job experience to completion of two years of approved courses.

## Professional Extenders

People in these jobs perform vital support services.

### Ophthalmic Registered Nurses

Ophthalmic registered nurses are relatively new to the field. They are registered nurses who have chosen to specialize in work with patients with vision problems. Their experience as operating room assistants has made them an invaluable addition to the staff of outpatient eye surgery centers.

### Allied Health Personnel

Ophthalmic and optometric allied health personnel are the assistants, technicians, technologists, and other professional extenders who provide a wide range of support services from greeting patients to grinding lenses to assisting in surgery. The preparation for their jobs ranges from on-the-job training to two or more years of postbaccalaureate education.

## Other Careers

Some eye care workers have extensive training and diverse experience that would allow them to work in almost any health care setting, but their choice of eye care is often a personal preference. Their roles are critical to patient care, although they may not be directly involved in its provision. These careers include ophthalmic researcher, photographer, administrator, and vision sciences librarian.

The roles of eye care practitioners may seem well defined. As you read further, you will see that there is a trend toward the blurring of the traditional boundaries in the scopes of practice. Eye care is a dynamic science, technology, and industry where new professions are added, and there are new opportunities for practitioners at every level.

Recently there have been dramatic changes in career roles as a result of increased economic competition and the availability of new technologies at almost every level of practice. Professionals are frequently competing for the same patients and are learning to market a wider range of services in more convenient locations to serve the eye care consumer.

## Why Choose Eye Care?

Throughout most of history, becoming a doctor, whether it involved a medical, osteopathic, or optometric degree, was a noble aspiration. However, today, when the need for health care professionals is increasing, there has been an alarming decline in the number of applicants to medical, osteopathic, and optometric schools. This is due to a change in young people's perceptions of the career when compared to the many other options for professional study. For example, lawyers and M.B.A.s can expect to spend less time in school, finish their education with less debt, make a higher starting and lifetime salary, and maintain a more reasonable work schedule and home life.

In an effort to encourage students to reconsider professional training in medicine, the associations that organize educational training for the medical professions have been very proactive in amending these perceptions. For example, the Association of Schools and Colleges of Optometry (ASCO) has developed a program called

"Each One, Reach One," in which practicing optometrists are encouraged to talk to their patients about entering their profession. And the website for the Association of American Medical Colleges (AAMC) has candid information about exploring careers in medicine—what it's really like—and a checklist to help you decide whether this is a career for you.

Before you go any further, ask yourself the following questions:

- Do I care deeply about other people, their problems, and their pain?
- Do I enjoy helping people with my skills and knowledge?
- Do I enjoy learning and gaining new understanding? Do I often dig deeper into a subject than my teacher requires? Do I understand the value of learning beyond just making good grades?
- Am I interested in how the human body functions? Am I intrigued by the ways medicine can be used to improve life?

If you answered "yes" to these questions, chances are you have the right kind of personality for a medical career or other vocation in eye care. There is also information on the AAMC website about a doctor's lifestyle, how to manage medical school debt, and how to prepare for and what to expect out of medical school. Similar information is available on the website for the American Association of Colleges of Osteopathic Medicine (AACOM). The website addresses for these organizations, as well as others involved in the promotion of allied eye care careers, can be found in Appendix A of this book.

Recently the eye care industry has been successful in attracting a diversified pool of aspiring professionals. There are many programs for people of any age, sex, or cultural background who seek a career in eye care, including financial aid for training. The Association of American Medical Colleges administers one of the most comprehensive programs. The goal of its Minority Medical Education Program (MMEP) is to offer promising students an all-expenses-paid, six-week summer program to interest them in medical education and to give them "a critical edge in the intense competition for medical school." The MMEP has been very successful, with 63 percent of its participants being accepted at medical schools.

Nowhere in the sections of this book that describe qualifications for various eye care careers will you find the statement "you must be a perfect human specimen." In fact, the health care field always has been in the forefront of training, hiring, and promoting disabled workers. As you read about the various career opportunities, imagine what it would take to accommodate a disabled worker: a closer parking space, barrier-free buildings, equipment that could be lowered, or communication devices such as TTD or Braille directional signs.

Many are the places where eye care workers have already made these changes for patients. There are few data on the number of disabled workers in the eye care field because disability doesn't matter as much as giving good patient care.

## Current Employment Outlook

The good news is that there are unlimited opportunities for people who enter the field of eye care ready to make a personal difference. Several positive factors are affecting eye care:

- Perhaps no other field of medicine is expanding as quickly in its knowledge of the disease process and in its use of technology to detect and correct problems.

• The world's population is expanding and living longer; there-fore, people who expect to be well and active into their senior years are demanding more and better eye care services.

• New types of jobs are being created as pressure from the gov-ernment and insurers to reduce the cost of eye care encourages providers to find creative ways of safely supplying services. For instance, the trend toward more same-day, outpatient surgery requires assembling a new team of very versatile care providers who can assure patients that this is a safe, more affordable, and accessi-ble option.

It is not surprising that the U.S. Bureau of Labor estimates that the need for workers in the eye care field will continue to expand more than the average for other health-related industries.

## Working Environment

Health care is often referred to as an *integrated delivery system.* This means that there are many different sets of health services provided by different types of personnel in different types of facilities, and all of these services are connected and interrelated. So, how does a patient know whom to see, for what, and where to go? Often, it is the patient's choice that determines where the services are provided and, subsequently, the locations of vision care workers' jobs.

Twenty years ago, the delivery system was less complicated. It was very doctor-centered. A patient went to the office of a family doctor during regular business hours for any health-related prob-lem. Emergencies were handled by the doctor making a house call. The doctor either treated the problem or sent the patient to a spe-cialist. All surgery was performed in hospitals. It was a simple system, but there was very little choice about which doctor to see, where to go, when to schedule an appointment, and how much the treatment would cost. Asking questions about your own health care options and participating in the medical decisions were discouraged.

Today, the patient chooses what doctor to see for a health problem. A first encounter with vision care could be at a health fair at the mall, where volunteers are administering vision-screening tests. Or a patient may receive regular vision screenings as part of an annual physical examination performed by the family doctor. Many patients are very well informed about vision care and choose to see an eye care professional such as an ophthalmologist or optometrist. Whomever they choose, this person is the patient's entry point into the complex, integrated network of eye care services. Although the modern system is complicated, patients have many choices of how, when, and from whom they wish to receive their eye care. There are so many factors that influence their decisions that today's patients are called *health care consumers*. For most consumers, the elements of cost, convenience, and satisfaction with the products and services they purchase are foremost in their decision making.

What are the implications for eye care workers? Their jobs are now focused on satisfying the patient/consumer, not the doctor. And speaking of the doctor, though still important, he or she is only one of a number of skilled professionals who work closely as part of a patient care team. Health care providers will be working in places and at times that patients find convenient, not necessarily regular business hours in the downtown office or hospital. They will be focused on giving patients good value for their dollars, which means cutting costs while still trying to make a living. And in a very competitive, integrated marketplace, they will be trying, at all levels of employment, to market services to new patients and find ways of keeping current patients happy. Why choose to work in eye care rather than sell new cars for a living? Because, what really makes a patient happy is caring, and doctors care. Patients will travel miles and spend more to be cared for by the people they trust with their precious eyesight. It is this environment that attracts people to eye care. Saving someone's sight is very satisfying work!

## How Convenience Has Shaped the Work Environment

In response to consumers' need for convenience, ophthalmologists have shifted to a "hospital without walls" concept. A good example is cataract surgery, which used to require several days of confinement in a big-city hospital. It is now done in a same-day surgery facility that may be an extension of the suburban group practice or part of the outpatient department of a small community hospital. The demand for technologists who can assist with outpatient ophthalmologic surgery has increased dramatically while the working conditions have improved.

Convenience also has had its effect on the optical marketplace. Small storefronts and optical shops run from converted garages have been made obsolete by huge superstores that are attached to shopping malls. Some huge chain stores, like Wal-Mart and Sears, also have large optical shops. A wide selection of fashionable frames and lenses, one-stop shopping for no-appointment eye exams, and one-hour turnaround on finished frames are services that are commonly advertised. To provide this type of high-volume service, the superstores employ large numbers of optometrists, opticians, and other technicians. In both the ophthalmic and optometric marketplace, being an employee on any level means being on the payroll of a large company. This means that there are often more opportunities for job advancement, more flexible schedules, more job security, and better benefits. In contrast, eye care workers who choose smaller office practices or clinics have more input into decision making, like the challenge of performing multiple tasks, and enjoy a closer relationship with patients and staff. This is a career path with lots of choices.

## How Cost Affects Eye Care

Cost has also been a major influence on the changes in the eye care delivery system. Eye care is now more available to almost every segment of the population because of the accessibility of health insurance. The government subsidizes eye care for the elderly and the disadvantaged through Medicare and Medicaid. Many working people receive vision care for themselves and their families as an employment benefit.

However, as increasing health care costs eat into the corporate bottom line, many companies have become very vocal about controlling medical costs. They often encourage their workers to enroll in health maintenance organizations (HMOs), which offer low-cost preventive health care as a means of deterring major illnesses and hospitalizations. This is called *managed care*, and it has been and will continue to be a major factor in shaping the economic working environment for eye care personnel. Eye care for HMO members usually includes low-cost periodic visits to specified providers— ophthalmologists or optometrists who have contracted with the HMO. Members are encouraged to have regular eye exams so that they can be monitored for serious eye diseases and receive immediate intervention while the chances of recovery are optimal. This type of care is extremely efficient because the member must use eye care providers who have agreed to accept the HMO's predetermined fee for treatment. The doctors and other eye care providers who work with HMOs and similar health insurance organizations are considered contractors. The arrangement is mutually beneficial since it provides a secure income for providers and controlled costs for employers and patients.

The conflict occurs when patients insist on expensive treatment options that may not be approved by the HMO. Experimental treatments for previously incurable diseases are especially controversial. Fortunately, HMO-insured patients can appeal to an arbitration panel that includes professional caregivers. Consequently, eye caregivers sometimes must face an ethical dilemma: what they may consider the best treatment option for a patient may also be the most costly. Nonetheless, they must balance this understanding with the "shared risk" principle of managed care, which is to ensure that everyone can receive care by rationing pieces of the health care "pie."

Managed care has caused health care organizations to be run more like businesses. Job opportunities are tied to a changing marketplace. As in other competitive industries, savvy workers constantly hone their skills with an eye toward making themselves marketable for a next career move. Concerns about longevity in one's job and loyalty to one's employer are values of the past. Twenty years ago, people chose health care careers, mostly in hospitals, because they were rewarding, well respected, secure, and provided a way to make a comfortable living. Doctors were very independent and considered wealthy. Today, the work is still rewarding and well respected, but incomes are variable and volatile just like in other types of businesses. Doctors have probably suffered the most. In some health occupations that are in short supply and high demand, such as nurse anesthetists, the salaries exceed those of doctors. Perhaps the saddest casualty of the "corporatization" of health care is job security. Hospital and health system layoffs, once unheard of, are now routine, making it hard for large city institutions to hire and retain skilled workers.

On the positive side, salaries and benefit packages for health care workers must be more competitive or these workers will go elsewhere. And the corporatization of health care has created many new types of businesses that need new types of workers.

## *What Has Happened to Hospitals?*

Does the movement toward outpatient eye care mean that there will be fewer jobs in hospitals? It's possible. One thing is for sure: the eye care occupations for hospital workers are getting more interesting. Since routine care can be provided in suburban offices and malls, hospitals have become true *tertiary care* centers. This means that hospitals are referral centers for problems that cannot be treated safely or effectively in the community. Eye care workers who choose the hospital setting face the challenge of applying cutting-edge knowledge and technology to the most difficult of cases. Often they are involved in researching new cures; they experiment with new equipment and techniques that are too expensive for private practices. Hospitals are still the best place to treat trauma victims, operate on high-risk patients with conditions like heart disease that might complicate eye surgery, or try an experimental treatment as a last resort to prevent blindness. They are still the best place for new professionals and technicians to train and learn to work well as a team.

One of the most exciting places to work in this field is an eye hospital. There are currently twenty eye hospitals in the United States that form a network of major research centers. The National Eye Institute coordinates much of the work that is pioneered at these facilities. The work environment is quite unique and appeals to those who welcome the most challenging of patient cases and have an interest in medical research and in educating many types of eye care professionals and workers. The eye hospitals are affiliated with major universities and medical schools. Teaching and learning are an important part of this very stimulating environment.

## *Mobile Practice Settings*

For those careerists who hate to be tied to an office, there are challenging opportunities in mobile screening and treatment units. Large vans that are equipped for vision testing and lens fitting bring care to rural communities, senior centers, nursing homes, and institutions. Some mobile units are sponsored by teaching institutions as a community outreach project, with the added benefit of providing hands-on experience for ophthalmic or optometric trainees.

Perhaps one of the most exciting opportunities in eye care is Project ORBIS. This converted DC-10 jet is truly a hospital without walls. The crew of ophthalmologists, nurses, and biomedical engineers has traveled to fifty cities on five continents since takeoff in 1982. Its mission is to exchange skills with and disseminate surgical techniques to other eye care professionals throughout the world. The plane has a complete state-of-the-art operating suite. Much of the teaching that takes place on board has to do with introducing local doctors to ambulatory surgery, which is still uncommon in many places. Providing eye care services on a plane presents some unique problems. For instance, all linen has to be disposable, since there is no water supply. ORBIS is an extraordinary opportunity for crew members to serve on a one-year rotation, acting not only as eye care practitioners, but also as diplomats.

## Challenges for Eye Care Workers

In health care, progress is a double-edged sword. With each advance, there is both the potential to do good and the potential to do harm. In a society where the expectation for a high level of technology clashes with the limited availability of resources, the boundaries between good and harm are often blurred. In a caregiving profession, the caregivers must have a strong sense of what is right and what is fair. This is what constitutes ethical behavior in the world of treatment and research. It is also the greatest intangible reward for choosing a career in health care—the knowledge that you leave the world a better place than you found it. But who gets to decide what is "better"?

As careful as health care workers are to protect the safety of patients, sometimes there are mistakes. When a patient suffers more from the medical treatment than the disease, a lawyer often steps in to try to win a monetary judgment for an injured client in a medical malpractice case. In some areas of the country, juries believe that huge payouts don't hurt anyone but the big insurance companies. In reality, the cost of malpractice awards has been passed on to doctors and other health care providers, causing them to leave their professions or move to states where the malpractice insurance premiums are more reasonable. In several states, the exodus of surgeons has caused a crisis. Although ophthalmology has not suffered as much as orthopedics or neurosurgery, the malpractice insurance crisis has discouraged some doctors from doing ophthalmic surgery.

A double-edged sword facing ophthalmologists these days is the increasing use of practice guidelines that are algorithms or formulas for providing cost-efficient care. Managed-care insurers are particularly interested in these formulas because they can result in a lower cost of care. Fortunately, many physicians who resent being told to use the cookbook recipe for patient care have applied their good medical research skills to not only looking for the cure of disease, but also to providing the safest process of treatment. In Canada, where national health care has been available to citizens for a long time, the Canadian Medical Association has taken an active role in compiling a database of physician-developed practice guidelines. The Medical Association has redefined practice guidelines as "systematically developed statements to help physicians and patients make decisions about appropriate health care in specific clinical circumstances."

Ophthalmic research is another area of ethical controversy. You have read about the future of ophthalmology and know that the science of genetics figures prominently in the elimination of vision-threatening diseases. But who decides that blindness is a human "defect" that should be eliminated? Think of the contributions of blind musicians, scientists, and humanitarians.

Using animals in biomedical research is also an ethical dilemma facing all scientists. Fortunately, there are guidelines for the humane treatment of research animals that are strictly enforced. But if you are opposed to animal research, you may want to avoid pursuing an eye care career that will require experimentation on the job or as part of your training.

Even with its unique challenges, eye care is still a career worth pursuing. This is one of the few areas of health care where the opportunities are very diverse and the relationship with patients is ongoing and rewarding.

# 2

---

# The Evolution and Future of Eye Care

It is difficult to pinpoint a particular date when eye care became a service that some people provided for others. The need to improve and preserve sight has always been related to the lengthening life span of human beings. But it is sometimes difficult to tell whether life is longer because of vision improvements or the opposite—that vision care progressed because a growing population of older people expected it.

The relationship between longevity and eyesight was clearer for the cave dwellers. Blindness was a death sentence. Their lives were filled with constant danger from wild animals, human enemies, and natural hazards. Primitive people who had poor vision died early in life because they could not protect themselves.

# A Brief History of Optics

In the first century A.D., Seneca recorded one of the first observations about refraction in his work *Questiones Naturales*: "Letters, however small and dim, are comparatively large and distinct when seen through a glass globe filled with water." Seneca's observation was only the beginning of humanity's attempts to understand eyesight.

Much of our knowledge of the origins of modern eye care comes from art and literature. Early pictures and writings of the Chinese and Romans show that vision remained a concern for centuries after prehistoric times. There is evidence that warriors, leaders, and explorers in these ancient societies wore some of the first eyeglasses. Marco Polo reported seeing spectacles on Chinese gentlemen and merchants in A.D. 1270. We also know that the Egyptians did eye surgery, because there are paintings depicting these operations.

The Chinese made their glasses from natural materials such as smoky quartz and rock crystals. The first manufactured lenses were made in the early fourteenth century in Venice, the cradle of modern glassmaking techniques. By the sixteenth century, the Italian astronomer Galileo focused on distant stars through the magnifying lenses of the first telescope.

## Colonial America

Eye care was not an advanced science in colonial America. Eye care for most American colonists consisted of making a decision about when to wear the eyeglasses passed down from generation to generation. Cataract surgery had not progressed significantly since the time of the ancient Greeks. Doctors who were interested in studying more about eye care trained in Europe and had to start their own hospitals because ophthalmology was not a recognized medical specialty. Spectacle makers were the only respected eye care professionals. Benjamin Franklin combined the glasses for both near and far vision in bifocal lenses.

Because they were rare and expensive, wearing spectacles was a sign of intelligence and wealth. President Thomas Jefferson wrote about his glasses:

> I received safely the spectacles and glasses you were so kind as to send me . . . and enclose you a 20 dollar bill on the bank of the U.S. the amount of their cost. The smallest pair of spectacles I am charmed with. They answer perfectly my wish. The other pair with double glasses I have not yet had time to try sufficiently and get them to fit my eye exactly. I have not doubt they will answer my expectation.

Fortunately, Mr. Jefferson was an inventor who knew how to tinker with corrective lenses. His inventions were only a portion of the accomplishments of his long and productive lifetime. It was his desire to stay active well into old age that fueled his expectations for counteracting age-related vision loss. Jefferson's fascination with extending the quality of his life with spectacles is a good example of how eye care has progressed.

## Modern Eye Care

Modern eye care probably began in the 1850s with the invention of the ophthalmoscope. As eye care specialists developed an understanding of the physiology of the eye and its relationship to other parts of the body, they needed instruments to help them examine the interior eye chamber without operating on the patient. There are two types of ophthalmoscopes that use light and mirrors to magnify the interior of the eye. This allows the eye examiner to view clearly the blood vessels, retina, and other parts of the eye interior and thus make an accurate diagnosis of a vision problem.

The ophthalmoscope heralded the twentieth century, known as the golden age of eye care. Early in the century, schools of optometry and ophthalmology proliferated. Eye surgery became safer, more effective as a treatment, and more accessible to middle-class patients. And by the 1960s, there were several internationally recognized eye institutes in America. These facilities were devoted exclusively to vision care, and they functioned as freestanding hospitals and research and training centers. The National Eye Institute was founded to coordinate the research that was making eye care so progressive. Many professional organizations, like the American Ophthalmologic Association, were founded to establish standards for certifying practitioners.

There is no doubt that eye care has evolved into a very complex system. It offers patients a wide range of choices. There are many types of professionals who are trained to administer care at various prices and in many locations. The scope of practices has also expanded to include not only care of the eye itself, but also parts of the body that interact with the eye to create vision. In other words, patients have to be good consumers. They have to know which doctor to see for a specific problem, where to locate good quality care, and how to pay for it.

In recent years, there has been some concern about the direction that eye care has taken. While eye care became a multifaceted form of health care, it also became a multibillion dollar industry. In response to concerns about the accessibility of quality eye care for average Americans, the U.S. Department of Health and Human Services, National Institutes of Health, included national objectives for vision care in its "Healthy Vision 2010" report. This report is considered a comprehensive blueprint for improving many aspects of the nation's health. The specific goals for eye care, outlined in "Healthy Vision 2010," are as follows:

## Overall Vision Goal

Improve the visual health of the nation through prevention, early detection, treatment, and rehabilitation

### *Vision Objectives*

- Increase the proportion of persons who have a dilated-eye examination at appropriate intervals
- Increase the proportion of preschool children aged five years and under who receive vision screening
- Reduce uncorrected vision impairment due to refractive errors
- Reduce blindness and visual impairment in children aged seventeen years and under
- Reduce visual impairment due to diabetic retinopathy
- Reduce visual impairment due to glaucoma
- Reduce visual impairment due to cataract
- Reduce occupational eye injury
- Increase the use of appropriate personal protective eyewear in recreational activities and hazardous situations around the home
- Increase the use of rehabilitation services and visual and adaptive devices by people with visual impairments

For the people who work in this field, these objectives are not new ones. "Healthy Vision 2010" is a way to focus the many resources of the vision care field, including education and research, on making a difference in the areas that will help the most people. For potential eye care workers, these priorities represent opportunities for present exploration, including volunteerism, as well as future job opportunities.

## A Glimpse into the Future

How will technology affect the future of eye care? Will eye care workers be replaced by robots? These are valid questions for the aspiring eye care professional who is about to invest a great deal of time and training in a rapidly changing occupation.

Today, our ideas about the future manifest themselves in movies and television shows like "Star Trek." In these futuristic scripts, people live to be hundreds of years old and solve their eye problems in ways that are unheard of today, but are fairly accurate depictions of future possibilities. One of the most popular "Star Trek" characters, Geordi LaForge, has been blind since birth. However, he sees better than most humans do with the use of a VISOR (Visual Instrument and Sensory Organ Replacement), the cumbersome futuristic glasses that transmit images to his brain. In the fictional year 2371, Geordi receives ocular implants that completely restore his vision. For Geordi and other "Star Trek" crew members, any type of medical treatment is quick and painless. The ship's doctors diagnose and treat their patients using small, handheld devices. All medical and surgical procedures are noninvasive—simply waving a device over the patient produces both the diagnosis and the cure. Here are a few predictions, from the medical literature, about eye care in the not-so-far-from-"Star Trek" future:

• Surgery will be the routine solution to many problems, eliminating the need for glasses and contacts.

• Surgical techniques will become less invasive, have fewer side effects, and take less time for both the operation and recovery. There will be less cutting and more innovative approaches to the manipulation of matter, such as the use of radio waves, heat, or cold.

• Implantation of devices other than lenses will continue to develop and will be used in conjunction with various types of surgery. Implantation of artificial visual devices to overcome blindness will be the ultimate goal.

• Time-released medications are already being developed, but in the future, they will be administered less frequently and will last longer. Time-released biodegradable pellets or small drug-releasing devices inserted in the eye will be particularly helpful to parents with small children or others who have difficulty with the administration of present-day forms of medications.

• Diagnostic testing will involve analyzing a patient's genetic predisposition for a particular problem and the tracking of minute changes in the body's physiology that are consistent with a disease process. Problems will be detected long before a patient fails to read an eye chart.

• Eye care professionals will shift from making patient-care decisions based on education and experience to using evidence-based medicine. They will choose among various treatment options by using clinical trials, computer-based systems that select relevant information from huge databases of literature, and other "expert" systems, including the analysis of cost-effectiveness.

High technology is becoming a part of everyday life, and the trend extends to eye care. Many of the most interesting careers in eye care can be found in the laboratories and hospital units where modern-day explorers investigate the scientific unknown territories of eye diseases.

You might wonder why there is so much research into the causes of blindness and ocular diseases. It is because knowing the cause is the basis of finding the cure. For this reason, a great deal of the research that is being conducted now and in the future is focused on genetics and the manipulation of genetic material to overcome inherited diseases and conditions such as *retinitis pigmentosa*. As the life expectancy of the average person increases, more research will focus on slowing all of the debilitating aspects of growing older, such as glaucoma. Perhaps one of the most fascinating prospects for the future is the combining of computer microchip technology with genetic engineering. Scientists speculate that some day we may swallow what looks like a pill, but is really a tiny microprocessor that seeks out genetic defects and corrects them. The ethics of what is a genetic "defect" may be more of a barrier to scientists than inventing the technology.

One serious threat to future progress is that government and private funding to research projects is shrinking. Although most people understand that our health care improves because of scientific research, a study conducted by the National Science Foundation showed that 98 percent of the people polled did not know where the money for research comes from. As a future eye care researcher, provider, or patient, it is important to be an activist for improved funding to this valuable endeavor.

Whatever the future holds, robots will never totally replace humans as eye care workers. We can be confident that there will always be a need for human contact. Even in the high-tech "sick bay" of the *Enterprise*, the patient sometimes needs to hold the doctor's hand. There is no replacement for the reassuring touch of a compassionate caretaker.

# 3

# OPHTHALMOLOGISTS

OPHTHALMOLOGY IS ONE of the oldest branches of medicine. Greek surgeons were successfully operating on cataracts during the classical era. Today, ophthalmology is one of the most technologically advanced—and one of the most diverse—of all medical specialties. Ophthalmologists are both medical and surgical doctors. Only two other medical specialties, obstetrics/gynecology and otolaryngology (ear, nose, and throat) combine primary care with surgery. Ophthalmologists can choose to concentrate their practices in a primary care setting, specialize in one very technical area of eye surgery, or offer a combination of skills. In addition to maintaining a clinical practice, many are affiliated with academic health centers where they enjoy teaching and doing research. Whether they may choose to work with children or adults, the rewarding, long-term relationships with their patients is what makes many aspiring doctors choose ophthalmology as a career.

## Career Description

An ophthalmologist is a physician (doctor of medicine or doctor of osteopathy) who specializes in the comprehensive care of the eyes and visual system. The ophthalmologist is the only eye care professional who is medically trained and qualified to diagnose and treat all eye and visual system problems. Ophthalmologists are different from optometrists and opticians, who are not physicians. Optometrists and opticians are much more limited in the types of diagnostic and treatment procedures that they can perform.

Some ophthalmologists choose to develop special expertise in a subspecialty within the medical specialty of ophthalmology. These are highly technical fields that require an extra two years of study and research at the fellowship level. The principal subspecialties of ophthalmology are:

Comprehensive ophthalmology
Corneal/extra-ocular disease
Glaucoma
Neuro-ophthalmology
Ophthalmic pathology
Ophthalmic plastic surgery
Pediatric ophthalmology
Vitreoretinal diseases

Areas of ophthalmology that have recently been recognized as new, emerging subspecialties include:

Contact lenses
Low-vision aids

Ophthalmic genetics
Ophthalmic oncology
Uveitis

The character traits of empathy and compassion are as necessary for the aspiring ophthalmologist as are intelligence and good judgment. Patients are often terrorized by the fear of going blind. Ophthalmologists must be skilled at dealing with the very stressful emotions that are involved in vision-threatening situations, and they must be able to build the trust that inspires a patient to stick with the therapy, even when the prognosis is grim.

Because an ophthalmologist is required to manipulate delicate instruments with precision, good fine-motor coordination, depth perception, and color vision are essential.

## Practice Settings

Ophthalmology, like most health care professions, has become an industry. This means that today's ophthalmologists must be concerned with more than just being good doctors. Twenty years ago, ophthalmologists were secure in their role as the most expert of the eye care providers. They were the only practitioners who were closely allied with hospitals. Most of the time, family doctors or optometrists referred patients to them. Ophthalmologists could expect to make a comfortable living by completing the required training and starting a practice.

In today's competitive environment, ophthalmologists are faced with competition from their former referral sources. Although they are still among the highest-paid eye care professionals, income has become a variable factor in a changing workplace, and the cost of running a practice, including malpractice insurance premiums, has increased dramatically.

Ophthalmologists still enjoy a great deal of geographic mobility and can find employment in almost every area of the country. Osteopathic ophthalmologists are generally located near osteopathic hospitals, which are concentrated in Florida, Michigan, Pennsylvania, New Jersey, Ohio, Texas, and Missouri.

Ophthalmology is still one of the most popular specialties among young doctors. Compared with other surgical specialties such as thoracic surgery or obstetrics, ophthalmology offers a reasonable lifestyle with above-average income. Unlike other doctors, ophthalmologists rarely have emergencies that call them into surgery. According to the American Academy of Ophthalmology, most ophthalmologists in general practice spend about four days in their offices and one day in the operating room. During a typical office day, an ophthalmologist will perform mostly medical diagnostic and treatment procedures. In a typical week, he or she will see approximately one hundred patients and perform two major surgical procedures. Most ophthalmologists work between thirty-five and fifty hours a week. Modern technology has made it possible to perform ophthalmic surgery in the doctor's office or surgical center.

## Solo and Group Practices

Most ophthalmologists are self-employed in private practices. However, as start-up costs increase, few young physicians see much future in going out on their own. Getting started now is likely to involve a less independent approach, such as:

- Buying an established practice
- Entering into an arrangement with a hospital

- Responding to recruiting by a rural community
- Sharing at least some facilities and functions with another colleague
- Cooperating with a number of other physicians in a "clinic without walls"

Pessimistic health care industry analysts predict that solo practice will be restricted to small towns and underserved areas. Rather than face the austerity of the start-up years, many young doctors will contract with hospitals and HMOs. Physicians in California and New Mexico have come up with solutions they think will help solo physicians and small group practices remain viable and independent. In both locations, physicians have formed their own corporations that provide a wide range of business services for doctors who want to remain in their own offices. The corporations pool expenses and achieve savings on purchases of equipment, medical supplies, bookkeeping and accounting services, health insurance premiums, and pension administration. Some groups even share office space, a receptionist, and medical technicians. In this "clinic without walls" scenario, a new ophthalmologist could share the overhead of starting a practice with physicians in other specialties or with other ophthalmologists. Although starting a private practice is risky, most doctors still believe that the personal freedom it affords makes it all worthwhile.

## Education and Training

Ophthalmologists are the most highly educated of the eye care professionals. They are expected to continue their education throughout their careers.

## Residency

To qualify for entry into an approved ophthalmology residency program, an applicant must have completed medical school, either as a medical doctor (M.D.) or as a doctor of osteopathy (D.O.), and have completed one year of postgraduate training, known as an internship or post-graduate year-one residency (PGY 1). The internship is usually not in ophthalmology, but in internal medicine, surgery, pediatrics, or a number of other disciplines. The competition for ophthalmology residency positions is intense. Applicants interview at many institutions hoping to be accepted at their first choice. In mid-March, residents and programs participate in a computerized "match" administered by the National Resident Matching Program, which provides an "impartial venue" for the pairing of residents with programs. After the match, the residents receive contracts from the programs outlining the conditions of their employment and training.

Residency training is one of the most rigorous parts of the ophthalmologist's training. The resident must see a large number and variety of patients to gain the experience needed for practice and board certification. It is often necessary for residents to rotate through several hospitals if they are to meet these requirements.

The resident's educational experience must be designed and supervised by the teaching program director. In the past, this training was described in terms of the hours and types of experiences. Today, residents must demonstrate that they have mastered several "competencies." These include:

• **Patient care.** This refers to the compassionate, appropriate, and effective treatment of health problems and the promotion of health.

- **Medical knowledge**. This means that the resident must have knowledge of the established and evolving biomedical, clinical, and cognate (for example, epidemiological and social-behavioral) sciences and know how to apply this knowledge to patient care.

- **Practice-based learning and improvement**. This requires that residents be involved in the investigation and evaluation of their own patient care and in the appraisal and assimilation of scientific evidence and improvements in patient care.

- **Interpersonal and communication skills**. This means that residents participate in effective information exchange and work with patients and their families.

These competencies are developed over a three-year period by combining classroom instruction with supervised hands-on experience, called clinical training. As the resident progresses, he or she becomes more independent in patient care responsibilities and takes on increasing responsibility for teaching and supervising more junior residents. In all types of residency training, including ophthalmology, the program director and the physicians who comprise the faculty are responsible for ensuring that the residents are progressing competently in their education and that in no way do they endanger the patients who are involved in their clinical experiences.

The classroom training consists of a minimum of 360 hours of education in the basic and clinical sciences and at least fifty hours of laboratory experience in gross and microscopic examination of pathological specimens. Strict attendance is kept at these sessions, which are conducted by the program's faculty and outside guest lecturers.

The outpatient experience for a resident during the three-year training program should consist of a minimum of approximately three thousand patient visits appropriately distributed through a broad range of ophthalmic disease in adults and children. The resident is expected to perform a substantial portion of each examination under the supervision of a faculty member.

In addition, residents perform and assist at sufficient surgery to become skilled as general ophthalmic surgeons. For example, each resident's experience typically includes a minimum of twenty-five cataract procedures and ten strabismus procedures, during which the resident has major technical and patient care responsibilities. Each resident has sufficient surgical experience—including laser surgery in cornea, glaucoma, retina/vitreous, oculoplastic, and trauma cases—to provide a solid base for general ophthalmic practice.

The work hours for residents are long when compared to other professions. However, for the health of the residents and the safety of their patients, their schedules are monitored to ensure that they do not spend more than eighty hours per week on patient care duties.

## Fellowships

Ophthalmic fellowships are for ophthalmologists who want to continue their education beyond residency to become experts in a subspecialty. Their hands-on training is generally focused on a particular type of patient or disease. They train at eye institutes or large universities where they are expected to participate in research projects, publish papers, and present at conferences in addition to caring for patients.

# Board Certification and Licensure

The distinction between board certification and licensing is often confusing. All practicing physicians, including ophthalmologists, must be licensed in the states where they see patients. Board certification is a voluntary credential, which shows the attainment of the highest level of knowledge and skills in the field of ophthalmology.

The purpose of the examinations given to ophthalmologists for board certification is to determine whether they have the knowledge, skills, and experience to provide patient care according to the high standards set by their profession. The American Board of Ophthalmology administers both the oral and written examinations. Passing the examinations means that the ophthalmologist is "board certified," a distinction all well-informed patients and referring physicians look for when choosing a specialist.

## *The Written Exam*

To qualify for an oral examination, each applicant must pass a written qualifying examination. This is a multiple choice test that may cover any topic in ophthalmology and is especially devoted to the following subjects from the basic and clinical science course of the American Academy of Ophthalmology:

- Optics, refraction, and contact lenses
- Retina, vitreous, and uvea
- Neuro-ophthalmology
- Pediatric ophthalmology and strabismus
- External disease and cornea

- Glaucoma, lens, and anterior segment
- Trauma
- Plastic surgery and orbital diseases
- Ophthalmic pathology

The written examination is given simultaneously in several cities in the United States in April of each year. An applicant who fails the written portion can repeat the test the following year.

## The Oral Exam

Upon successful completion of the written exam, applicants receive instructions for taking the oral part. Oral examinations are held twice annually at a time and place determined by the board. A panel of examiners gives the oral exam during a one-day period. The examination is divided into six sections, and the emphasis is placed upon recognition of depicted or described abnormalities and diseases that affect the eye, ocular adnexa, and the visual pathways, and upon the ability of the candidate to synthesize clinical, laboratory, and histopathologic data to arrive at a correct diagnosis. Candidates are expected to provide a reasonable and appropriate plan for medical and/or surgical management of the hypothetical patient. These examinations include developmental, dystrophic, degenerative, inflammatory, infectious, toxic, traumatic, neoplastic, and vascular diseases affecting the eye and its surrounding structures.

Candidates are expected to be competent in the following subjects:

1. **Optics, refraction, and visual physiology**. Candidates should understand the essentials of visual physiology, including

visual acuity, light and dark adaptation, accommodation and color vision, various forms of ametropia, principles and techniques of refraction, principles of lens design, and methods of correction of ametropia with glasses and contact lenses. They should be familiar with the methods for prescribing protective lenses, absorptive lenses, and aids for low vision.

2. **Pediatric ophthalmology and strabismus.** Candidates are expected to understand the anatomy and physiology of the neuromuscular mechanisms subserving ocular motility and binocular vision. They should be familiar with the methods of examination for detection and assessment of sensory and ocular motor disorders. They also should know the clinical features, differential diagnosis, natural course, and management of the various types of deviations. They should be familiar with principles and complications of surgery upon the extraocular muscles.

3. **Neuro-ophthalmology and orbit.** Candidates will be examined on the principles and techniques of various diagnostic procedures, including visual field testing, visual evoked responses, ultrasonography, conventional x-ray imaging, CT scanning, and magnetic resonance imaging. Candidates should be familiar with the clinical features, pathology, differential diagnosis, and management of various disorders of the orbit, visual pathways, oculomotor systems, and pupillomotor pathways, including the indications for, principles of, and complications of orbital surgery.

4. **External eye and adnexa.** Candidates should know the anatomy, embryology, and physiology of the structures comprising the lacrimal system, lids, conjunctiva, and anterior sclera. They should demonstrate knowledge of the pathology, diagnosis, and therapy as well as indications, principles, and complications of surgical procedures to alleviate abnormalities and diseases affecting these tissues.

5. **Anterior segment of the eye.** This includes the anterior chamber angle, iris, ciliary body, and lens.

6. **Posterior segment of the eye.** This includes the vitreous, retina, choroid, and posterior sclera.

There are two additional sections of the examination that test the candidate's knowledge of the anatomy, embryology, physiology, and pathology of abnormalities and diseases of the eye. Candidates are expected to discuss conditions affecting these structures and those to be considered in differential diagnosis. They also should be able to describe and provide indications for medical and surgical therapies directed toward alleviating or curing these various conditions.

## Certification

Board certification is good for ten years, at which time an ophthalmologist must present proof of participation in continuing education programs and be in good standing with his or her state licensing board.

## Licensing

Every state in the United States has a medical licensing board that reviews the applications of health practitioners who would like to provide patient care within its jurisdiction. An ophthalmologist who has completed his or her residency and who is board certified or eligible to take the boards must fill out an application that is submitted to the licensing board. All of the information, including medical school attendance, residency training, and references from hospitals and other doctors, is checked by the state licensing board. The board will also query the National Practitioner Databank, which is a federally mandated program that compiles information on physicians who have had problems such as hospital suspensions, revoked licenses in other states, excessive malpractice cases, or other issues with the quality of care provided to their patients. When all of the information is verified as correct and the physician is deemed qualified to practice in the state, a license is issued and must be renewed on a regular basis. Ophthalmologists, like other physicians, must show that they have participated in the amount of continuing education that is required by the state for re-licensing. For ophthalmologists, education is a lifelong pursuit.

Licensed by the state to practice medicine and surgery, an ophthalmologist is the only provider who can deliver total eye care. This care includes diagnosis of diseases of the eye and other bodily systems; comprehensive vision service, including prescribing medications, therapy, and corrective eyeglasses and contact lenses; and medical and surgical eye care.

## Compensation and Employment Outlook

Recent statistics from the American Medical Association showed that ophthalmology is still a popular choice among physicians. In the AMA's data on the distribution of physicians in thirty-six recognized specialties, ophthalmology was listed as the thirteenth-largest group of doctors. Among the nine surgical subspecialties, ophthalmology ranked third behind general surgery and orthopedics. There are currently about fifteen thousand ophthalmologists in the United States.

The average income of an ophthalmologist currently ranges from about $165,000 to $223,000 based on a number of variables including location, size, and maturity of the practice. After years of steady gain in both income and growth in numbers, some experts believe that the ophthalmology market has peaked. Medicare reimbursement for cataract surgery, the most popular of all surgical procedures, has been reduced several times in the past few years. Although the government has recommended additional reductions in many ophthalmologic treatments, lobbying efforts by ophthalmologists' professional associations have managed to mitigate these attempts and increase reimbursement. Private insurers and HMOs, following Medicare's lead, have reduced reimbursement to ophthalmologists as well. In addition to reductions in income, ophthalmologists have also had tremendous increases in expenses, particularly in the area of malpractice insurance. Many ophthalmologists have joined a malpractice plan organized by the American Academy of Ophthalmology to try to reduce these costs.

The demand for ophthalmologists is expected to increase as the population ages. Demand will be greatest in rural and typically underserved areas. Some trends that will negatively impact on the demand for ophthalmologists are the recent technological advances that have eliminated the need for surgery, and in many states, the scope of practice for optometrists has been broadened to overlap that of their M.D. colleagues. Patients who are insured through managed-care plans are also sometimes denied access to specialists, like ophthalmologists, and must be referred by their primary care physician, who is encouraged by the insurance plans to perform basic eye care.

On the supply side, there are fewer new graduates and, although there is the tendency among many older physicians to work beyond traditional retirement age, ophthalmologists, like surgeons, lose their dexterity as they age. In short, if new ophthalmologists are flexible about where they work, they can do very well.

Ophthalmologists are finding creative ways of counteracting negative market influences. One strategy uses the "if you can't beat them, join them" philosophy. Integration of the full spectrum of eye care services at one location is what patients want and what ophthalmologists are delivering. These services run the gamut from primary eye care through state-of-the-art ambulatory surgery. Some ophthalmologists network with neighboring optometrists; others acquire optometric practices and employ the former owners in order to eliminate the competition. The larger centers that can offer more services at lower cost can contract with managed-care insurers to further ensure a large patient base.

Many doctors have objected to advertising in the past. However, optical superstores have been so aggressive in this arena that ophthalmologists must use all media, including direct mail, to court patients and referring physicians. Websites describing the services and expertise of the staff and offering consumer information on eye problems and treatments are another popular marketing tool used by ophthalmologists.

Ophthalmologists have long been advocates of using physician extenders, such as ophthalmic technicians, to increase the productivity and profitability of a practice. As the scope of services offered by the practice broadens, the opportunities for paraprofessional workers expand.

Finally, as the general public becomes better educated about the distinctions among the professional roles of eye care providers, ophthalmologists hope to see an influx of patients who understand the value of seeing a medical specialist for a serious problem. Outreach programs such as Prevent Blindness America have been very effective in making people more aware of the risks of eye disease and the benefits of early intervention and good quality care. As public awareness grows, many people will have a better understanding of why and when to see an ophthalmologist.

# 4

# OPTOMETRISTS

As DISCUSSED IN the previous chapter, ophthalmology is a medical specialty and ophthalmologists are medical and surgical doctors. However, for most people in America who wear glasses or contact lenses, their "eye doctor" is a doctor of optometry, commonly called an *optometrist*.

## Career Description

Optometrists are specialists who are trained and licensed to diagnose and treat more than one thousand ocular conditions and who are qualified to screen for many eye diseases. At the moment, what distinguishes this "eye doctor" from an ophthalmologist is that the optometrist does not perform surgery. However, as in other medical professions, the differences between practitioners blur as the public demands more accessible services and state licensing boards respond by expanding the privileges of medical caregivers. Currently, optometrists also differ from opticians, who make and dispense the lenses prescribed by optometrists. However, in the near future, it is possible that the states will further confuse these roles by licensing "refracting opticians," who will prescribe lenses just like optometrists do.

As in the other eye care professions, the optometrist's scope of practice has expanded, most recently with the addition of privileges to prescribe and administer optometric drugs. Typical functions performed by an optometrist include:

- Using instruments and observation to examine eye health
- Checking for visual acuity and depth and color perception
- Evaluating the patient's ability to focus and coordinate the eyes
- Developing a treatment plan to correct vision problems
- Prescribing corrective eyeglasses, contacts, vision therapy, and low-vision aids
- Administering drugs for diagnosis and treatment of eye diseases, including prescribing drugs for patients
- Diagnosing systemic diseases such as diabetes or hypertension that are detected in the eye
- Referring patients who require special treatment to appropriate specialists, such as ophthalmologists or other consultants
- Providing pre- and postoperative care to eye surgery patients
- Teaching, engaging in research, or consulting

Optometrists, like ophthalmologists, may choose to limit their practice to a specialty that focuses on a particular patient population or type of care. Some industry experts predict that these optometric specialties will be the roles of the optometrist of the future, if opticians gain privileges to perform refractions. They also believe that these specialties offer the most opportunities for solo practice for those optometrists who are just starting their careers and would like to practice in a one-person setting.

## *Low-Vision Optometry*

Low-vision optometrists work in conjunction with ophthalmologists, social workers, and government and private agencies to provide vision aids to people who cannot see with conventional eyeglasses or contact lenses. These patients are often considered legally blind, and their vision cannot be corrected using standard refraction methods. The optometrist's role on this team is to design optical devices such as laser canes and various types of magnifiers and illuminators. These adaptive devices improve the quality of life for low-vision clients by making it possible for them to work, go to school, and enjoy leisure activities like watching television. They also help with other conditions such as:

• **Binocular vision.** Crossed eyes or eyes that do not work together are a common symptom of patients who are treated by low-vision optometrists. These experts prescribe special devices, eyewear, and exercises.

• **Vision therapy.** Patients who work with a vision therapist have problems with eye movements such as focusing and tracking, among others. They might also have difficulty processing visual information.

• **Sports therapy.** Optometrists specialize in all aspects of improving the visual aspects of athletic performance, including recommending safety eyewear.

- **Head trauma.** These specialists assist accident and stroke victims with their vision-related recovery.

- **Environmental and occupational vision.** These consultants give advice on how to prevent eyestrain in the workplace and make recommendations for safe practices to prevent eye injuries.

- **Learning disabilities or developmental vision.** One of the less-well-known, yet fascinating, branches of optometry is developmental vision. This is the study of how eyesight is related to human behavior. Optometrists who specialize in this field frequently work with pediatricians, child psychologists, educators, and social workers to diagnose and treat learning disorders like dyslexia. Optometrists use their special training in eye-hand and other vision-related sensory-motor coordination to guide young patients into a lifestyle that enables them to succeed at school and participate in sports and the other activities enjoyed by their peers. Developmental vision specialists frequently work with strabismus and amblyopic patients to help these patients overcome vision problems. The relationship that evolves between the developmental optometrist, the patient, and other members of the interdisciplinary treatment team is very rewarding.

## Infant and Pediatric Optometry

Optometrists who specialize in the care of infants treat conditions that occur in the first four years of life. Pediatric optometry is a popular specialty. It is estimated that 20 percent of the children between the ages of five and nine and over 30 percent of the children from fifteen to nineteen have vision problems. Myopia, amblyopia, and strabismus are common conditions that afflict children.

Pediatric optometrists are trained to work with a child and his or her parents to correct these conditions through training and therapy. The optometrist often utilizes advanced techniques in biofeedback and nutrition counseling to ensure that children receive optimal care and to overcome the problems that interfere with therapy compliance. Recently, pediatric optometrists have been working with the babies of drug-addicted parents. Vision deficits are a common birth defect among this population.

## Geriatric Optometry

On the other end of the age spectrum is geriatric optometry. Many of these specialists spend all or part of their time working in nursing and retirement homes. Almost all of the elderly have vision problems. An optometrist who has chosen to work with this population must be well acquainted with the ocular manifestations of age-related diseases, such as eye problems caused by diabetes. Since many elderly people take a variety of prescription drugs, the geriatric optometrist also must be an expert on how to detect the ocular side effects of a patient's medications. He or she must know how to screen for eye diseases like glaucoma and cataracts that are more prevalent among the elderly and require timely intervention by an ophthalmologist. Optometrists frequently work with ophthalmologists to provide postoperative monitoring and care after procedures like cataract extractions. Many nursing and retirement homes have wellness centers that are specially equipped for the visiting optometrist. In some areas, the optometrist has equipped a van as a mobile unit. This enables the optometrist to offer complete care wherever he or she goes. Good optometric care is an important factor in providing the best quality of life for older people, who now expect to be active well into their retirement years.

### Cornea and Contact Lenses

With more than fourteen million people wearing contact lenses, some optometrists have limited their practices to fitting contact lenses. The popularity of extended wear and tinted lenses has significantly increased the demand for optometrists who specialize in this field. In addition to regular contact lenses, optometrists are trained to design very specialized lenses. *Orthokeratology* is the practice of using a series of progressively flatter contact lenses to gradually reshape the cornea and reduce myopia. Some optometrists choose the subspecialty of pediatric contact lenses. Teaching children to insert and care for their lenses is a special talent that these optometrists have mastered in addition to the complexity of fitting young patients. Contact lens specialists, because they have seen more patients with particular types of complications, are experts on the infections, irritations, and other problems related to wearing contact lenses. They are often hired as consultants to the lens manufacturing industry to assist in the design of more comfortable and problem-free products.

## Practice Settings

It is difficult to determine how the "average" optometrist spends the day. Of all the eye care careers, optometry may have the widest range of business structures and the most fluid practice boundaries. Twenty years ago, most optometrists were easily characterized. They prescribed and fit conventional lenses from small shops that they owned and operated during business hours. Their patients came from the surrounding community, and the practice, which was based on caring and good quality service, grew from word-of-mouth referrals.

Like ophthalmologists, optometrists work in a variety of settings. The number of optometrists has declined by several thousand in the last few years, leaving a workforce of about thirty-one thousand practitioners. About three quarters of those are in private practice and about half are in solo practices. Other practice settings include:

- Partnerships or group practices
- Health Maintenance Organizations (HMOs)
- Multidisciplinary physician teams
- Specialized hospitals and eye clinics
- Retail optical stores
- Military or public health
- Academic pursuits or research in university settings
- Corporate research laboratories or clinics
- Consultants to industry, education, sports, and government
- Multidisciplinary teams working with patients who are learning disabled

Today's optometrist has many choices of work environments. The options range from working as a part-time employee to owning a chain of franchised superstores. An optometrist's customers are very sophisticated shoppers who are looking for one-stop convenience and respond to the flashy advertising that prompts them to shop for fashion rather than quality. Some optometrists believe that their profession has suffered from the public's misperception of their roles. Patients expect their optometrist to dispense eyewear that is competitively priced with optical chain stores, and they forget that they are receiving the services of a highly trained and experienced professional. Although an optometrist may be committed to personalized, quality care, he or she also must make a living in a very competitive marketplace.

A few things about the optometry workplace are still standard. Most optometrists still do work about a forty-hour week. Those who are in private practice work more hours. Working hours normally begin between 8:00 and 10:00 A.M. and end between 4:00 and 9:00 P.M. Some evening and weekend hours are necessary to accommodate patients. Now that optometrists can prescribe medications, they are accepting emergency calls as well.

The work is not physically strenuous, but it does require manual dexterity, making it an ideal career for someone who intends to be active into what might be considered traditional retirement years. Successful optometrists tend to be analytical thinkers who understand the importance of integrating knowledge of new scientific and technological developments with established diagnostic and treatment methods.

In recent years, optometrists have become more holistic in their approach to eye care. A more in-depth look at the patient's medical condition and history gives the optometrist more insight into the cause of vision problems. Optometrists are taking a broader approach to treatment as well. In addition to prescribing corrective lenses, an optometrist might suggest nutrition therapy or consultation with a geriatrician about vision-related medication side effects in the elderly.

Jobs are available in most areas of the country, although nearly half of all optometrists work in California, Illinois, New York, Ohio, and Pennsylvania.

## Education and Training

Graduation from high school or completion of an equivalency program is a prerequisite for all optometric training. Most pre-optometry students then complete a bachelor's degree program that should include the courses required for entry to most optometry graduate schools:

- General biology with labs
- General chemistry with labs
- Organic chemistry/biochemistry with labs
- General physics with labs
- Microbiology with labs
- Calculus
- Psychology
- Statistics
- English
- Social science
- Other humanities

Competition for admission to optometry school is keen, and applicants are evaluated at a personal interview and on their college grade point average, on an essay about themselves, and on their score on the Optometric Admissions Test (OAT). Some exposure to the field of optometry is considered desirable, and a recommendation from a practicing optometrist is a real bonus.

Optometry school is a four-year postgraduate program leading to a doctorate degree. The curriculum at each school or college varies somewhat, but each program follows a similar sequence of courses leading to the doctor of optometry degree.

In the first and second years, students concentrate on the basic health sciences including anatomy, physiology, pathology, biochemistry, pharmacology, public health, and preliminary training in optics and vision science. Their clinical training consists of "simulating" patient care with their fellow classmates by taking case histories, performing examinations and diagnostic tests, and formulating treatment plans. In the third year, students continue their classroom work, but begin to examine actual patients at the school's clinic. The fourth year includes extensive clinical training and may involve taking outside rotations at hospitals, military facilities, and private or specialty practices.

Most schools offer preceptorships or internships, during which experienced "teaching optometrists" will supervise fourth-year students as they provide hands-on care in various practice settings. Most optometry colleges provide a vital community service by operating clinics where their students are exposed to the unique problems of nursing-home patients, inner-city neighborhood health-clinic patients, inmates at correctional facilities, institutionalized or underserved blind patients, and visually impaired patients.

Like ophthalmology residents, optometry residents are expected not only to pass courses, but also to master a list of competencies known as *functional standards*. The Association of Schools and Colleges of Optometry (ASCO) developed these requirements and recommends that prospective students review the competencies before considering the profession. The functional standards in optometry education require that the student possess abilities in the following areas:

- Observation
- Communication
- Sensory and motor coordination
- Intellectual-conceptual, integrative, and quantitative abilities
- Behavioral and social attitudes

Students are expected to demonstrate that they have mastered a list of very specific behaviors that accompany each standard.

Optometry school is rigorous training, and it culminates in the student's receiving the doctor of optometry degree. However, having the O.D. is not enough to begin practice. Almost all states require that optometrists pass a written examination before becoming licensed to practice. This test is sometimes given during the final years of optometry school to test the student's comprehension of preparatory courses and his or her readiness to practice. Optometrists who are relocating their offices from one state to another can, generally, transfer their license without taking the examination.

Following graduation and licensing, most optometrists go into a community practice. Those who are academically inclined continue their education by completing a master's or doctorate degree in a related discipline such as visual science, physiological optics, neurophysiology, public health, health administration, health education, or a number of other specialties. Many of those who seek advanced degrees go on to teach or perform research.

For those optometrists who would like to limit their practices to a particular specialty within optometry, there are one-year residencies in family practice, pediatrics, geriatrics, low-vision rehabilitation, vision training, hospital-based optometry, and primary-care optometry.

## Board Certification and Licensure

The National Board of Examiners in Optometry (NBEO) develops and administers the national boards for optometrists. It is a comprehensive examination that consists of three parts: basic science, clinical science, and patient care. The exam is given twice a year and lasts for two and half days. The patient care section is conducted over a weekend so that examiners can observe the applicant one-on-one as he or she progresses through a five-station performance laboratory. At each station, the applicant must examine a patient while the examiner evaluates not only technical skills, but also clinical habits and attitudes. A written examination on patient assessment and management takes three and half hours to complete. The national boards are intended to test an applicant's readiness for optometric practice. Once certified, an optometrist must periodically renew his or her board certification by submitting documentation that shows that the board's standards for continuing education have been met. In addition to the comprehensive board exams, the NBEO develops and administers exams to test the advanced knowledge of practicing optometrists. Several years ago, a special examination was developed for certification on the Treatment and Management of Ocular Diseases, also known as TMOD. This certification is required by most state licensing boards to allow optometrists to administer and prescribe therapeutic drugs.

As in other health careers that require state licensure, passing the professional board examination can be substituted for the state's written examination. In thirteen states, optometrists are also required to take an additional examination regarding legal statutes that govern optometric practice in that state. Licensure procedures for optometrists are similar in other ways to that of other health care professionals. They must submit an application that details their education, training, and experience. Licensure must be renewed periodically by reapplying and submitting information on continuing education. An optometrist's license can be revoked or denied if it can be proved that he or she has been incompetent or guilty of misconduct.

## Compensation and Employment Outlook

The demand for optometrists is expected to increase at the same rate as all occupations through the year 2010. As previously noted, there are currently about thirty-one thousand practicing optometrists. According to the American Optometric Association, 40 percent under the age of forty are women and about 13 percent are minorities. A recent compensation survey by the AOA showed a wide range of salaries. The average income for optometrists in 2000 was $138,846. This was also about the average salary of solo practitioners. Income increased in proportion to the size of the practice. Practitioners in mid-sized (three-to-five person) practices earned some of the highest salaries ($182,397). The lowest salaries were among those optometrists who were employed by large retail chains ($116,071).

A major factor that will influence the increasing need for optometrists is the aging of the American public. There are many new, appealing optical products for the baby boomer, such as progressive lenses (no telltale bifocal line) and contact lenses that correct presbyopia. Almost all elderly people need some sort of vision correction, and because they are at risk, elderly patients must be examined frequently for many common eye diseases. Among the aging population are the many baby-boomer optometrists. Although this is an occupation that allows people to continue working beyond the traditional retirement age, some optometrists will choose to sell their practices to new entrants to the field.

Other factors that are expected to influence the demand for optometrists include the following:

- Shrinking enrollment at optometry schools may force them to affiliate with universities that have more resources for recruitment and financial aid.
- Although managed-care insurers have reduced the reimbursement for the optometrist's services, patients have more expendable income and are willing to spend it on fashionable eyewear.
- State regulatory agencies that once were considered restrictive now may support optometry by requiring mandatory eye exams for children entering school and for drivers renewing their licenses.
- State licensing boards have started granting privileges to specially trained optometrists to perform laser surgery.
- Even though laser procedures like LASIK are becoming safer and more popular, many patients either cannot afford them or prefer more noninvasive options like refraction.
- Some experts believe that the profits have peaked for the large retail chains and that these chains will continue to merge to acquire larger segments of the discount market.
- Starting a solo practice will become more difficult, but it may be a viable option for specialists. Small group practices with multiple locations will be the structure of the future.

With half of the population wearing corrective lenses, optometry should be a career choice with lots of opportunities for the future.

# 5

---

# OPTICIANS

OF THE THREE O's of eye care at the professional level (ophthalmologists, optometrists, and opticians), opticians have one of the most difficult jobs in eye care—ensuring that the patient's vision is actually improved by carrying out the directive of the "eye doctor," an optometrist or ophthalmologist. As we have seen in other eye care professions, the scope of practice for opticians is changing. Sometime in the near future, it is likely that opticians, like optometrists and ophthalmologists, will perform vision testing and prescribe refraction.

## Career Description

As in the other eye care professions, opticians can specialize in particular areas of their work. In general there are two main types of opticians: dispensing opticians and manufacturing opticians, more commonly known as optical laboratory technicians. Although some of their training and duties are similar, dispensing opticians work with patients to select eyewear, and manufacturing opticians work behind the scenes to grind prescription lenses and insert them in eyeglass frames.

Members of this profession are very concerned about the public's perception of the quality of their work, and they have established certifications for the various types of opticians and accreditation for their schools and training programs. The Commission on Opticianry Accreditation (COA), which is recognized by the U.S. Department of Education as the official accrediting body for optician training programs, defines the two major professional roles as follows:

## Ophthalmic Dispensing Optician

Ophthalmic dispensing opticians are broadly defined as those individuals who adapt and fit corrective eyewear as prescribed by the ophthalmologist or optometrist. Upon completion of their training, ophthalmic dispensing opticians should, at the minimum, be able to:

- Use effective oral and written communication
- Perform basic algebra, trigonometry, and geometry
- Identify the human eye structure, function, and pathology
- Determine physiognomic (facial and eye) measurements
- Neutralize eyewear/vision aids prescriptions
- Assess vocational and avocational needs of the consumer/patient
- Assist the consumer/patient in selecting proper frames and lenses
- Price and collect fees from consumers/patients for vision aids and services

- Prepare ophthalmic laboratory job orders
- Deliver prescription eyewear/vision aids and instruct consumer/patient in their use and care
- Maintain consumer/patient records
- Provide follow-up service to consumer/patient, including periodic eyewear/ophthalmic device adjustment, repair, lens and frame replacement
- Respond to ophthalmologist/optometrist complaints
- Apply rules and regulations for safe work practices
- Demonstrate proficiency in the operation and function of equipment
- Utilize and maintain equipment
- Demonstrate proficiency in finishing techniques
- Explain theory of refraction
- Assist in the business-related area of opticianry, including record maintenance, frame and lens inventory, supply and equipment maintenance, and third-party forms
- Demonstrate principles of adaptation, dispensing, and fitting contact lenses
- Identify procedures associated with dispensing artificial eyes and low-vision aids, when appropriate
- Discuss prescription eyewear/vision aids and other consumer/patient related information (verbal and written) with the prescriber

## *Ophthalmic Laboratory Technician*

The ophthalmic technician is an individual who grinds and polishes lenses and fabricates eyewear. His or her wide range of duties includes transcribing prescriptions, selecting appropriate lens forms, and processing the materials to the desired prescription. In addition, duties may include contact with other opticianry professionals as well as optical suppliers. Upon completion of their training, ophthalmic laboratory technicians should, at the minimum, be able to:

- Use effective oral and written communication
- Maintain consumer/patient records
- Perform basic mathematical and algebraic operations
- Prepare ophthalmic laboratory job orders
- Assess vocational and avocational needs of the consumer/patient
- Select proper frames and lenses for job orders
- Utilize and maintain equipment
- Respond to dispenser's complaints
- Apply rules and regulations for safe work practices
- Demonstrate proficiency in the operation and function of equipment
- Assist in the business-related area of ophthalmic laboratory technology, including record maintenance, frame and lens inventory, supply and equipment maintenance
- Neutralize eyewear/vision aids prescriptions
- Perform final inspection and verification
- Surface, grind, and polish lenses
- Fabricate eyewear
- Tint and coat lenses
- Perform minor frame repair
- Perform impact-resistance treatment and testing
- Discuss prescription eyewear/vision aids and other consumer/patient related information (verbal and written) with the prescriber

Most people think that selecting eyeglass frames is a matter of personal taste. Opticians know that there are more considerations than just style. Information about the patient's line of work, recreational activities, and lifestyle are factored into the choice, as well as hair coloring and facial features. The weight and thickness of lenses sometimes limits the choices. The tools of the optician's trade are optical pliers, files, and screwdrivers—as well as good judgment, tolerance, and tact.

Some opticians specialize in fitting artificial eyes or cosmetic shells for disfigured eyes. These specialists are called *ocularists*. Other opticians become more generalized by becoming experts in nonprescription optical goods like binoculars, magnifying glasses, sunglasses, and recreational or industrial eye protectors.

## Practice Settings

Most opticians work in very pleasant surroundings. Dispensing opticians may work in small offices with optometrists or ophthalmologists or in retail optical shops in department stores or malls. Some experienced opticians own their own optical shops, although this has become difficult in a very competitive marketplace. Laboratory technicians (manufacturing optometrists) can work in a variety of settings. In a small laboratory, a single technician performs all phases of the work. In a larger manufacturing company, the process is a highly automated assembly line and the technician might operate a machine that is very specialized. Most opticians work forty to fifty hours a week. Those who work in a retail setting often work on weekends and a few evenings a week.

The working conditions in both shops and laboratories are comfortable. The work is not physically demanding, although dispensing opticians can spend a lot of time on their feet and laboratory technicians must be able to operate various types of equipment. In fact, this is an occupation that is well suited to older workers or those who are physically handicapped but have the use of their hands and eyes.

Opticians must have people skills. The patients who have contact with dispensing opticians are generally relaxed and pleasant to deal with; they are not in pain or anticipating surgery, as might be the case of ophthalmologists' patients. The dispensing optician's interpersonal skills must also include the ability to transact the sales of eyewear. Laboratory technicians, especially those working in larger establishments, must be "team players" who are willing to do what is necessary to work efficiently and safely with coworkers. The equipment and raw materials (glass, chemicals) they work with can be hazardous, so they must be aware of and observe special safety precautions.

## Education and Training

Although there are several different paths that lead to professional opticianry, most people start with on-the-job training before pursuing formal occupational education. Those who go on to complete the educational program from an accredited school are in the most demand and command the highest salaries. These programs are approved by the Commission on Opticianry Accreditation and are offered by many community colleges and vocational and trade schools. The college programs lead to an associate's degree. A list of these schools can be found in Appendix C.

Applicants for formal ophthalmic dispensing programs must be high school graduates. Preference is given to students who are proficient in math, general sciences, physics, algebra, geometry, and mechanical drawing. Previous experience in a sales or public services job is also desirable.

Course work for the two-year college program generally includes combinations of the following topics:

### Profession-Related Courses

Assessment of the visual system
Business management
Contact lens clinical experience (internship or externship)
Contact lens fitting
Contact lens modification
Contact lens theory
Dispensing clinical experience (internship or externship)
Dispensing theory
Fabrication techniques
Geometric optics
Ocular anatomy, physiology, and pathology
Ophthalmic materials
Ophthalmic optics
Ophthalmic terminology
Opticianry sales techniques
Patient/customer/client relationships
Prescription analysis
Production and quality control methods
Professional ethics
Relationships with eye care professionals and laboratory
    personnel
Safety and environmental health
Scope of practice

Spectacle fitting and adjusting
State and national opticianry regulations

*General Education Content Areas*
Behavioral science
Computer technology
English
Mathematics
Science

Of the twenty-one states that license opticians, nineteen accept graduation from a COA-accredited program in lieu of the old standard that required an apprenticeship. Students who attend these programs are also eligible for federal funding, student loans, and scholarships.

Another career pathway is through the large optical chains. People with an interest but no experience in optical work can enroll. Although there is some classroom work, most of the training comes through an on-the-job apprenticeship. In addition to technical training, the apprentices also are instructed on office management, sales, and marketing. They have opportunities to increase their technical expertise by participating in seminars conducted by manufacturers, like the contact lens producers, or by attending special continuing education courses offered by medical schools or professional associations. Most apprenticeship programs last from two to four years.

Nearly all ophthalmic laboratory technicians learn their skills on the job. Employers filling entry-level jobs prefer applicants who are high school graduates. Courses in science and mathematics are valuable, and the ability to do precision work is essential.

Entry-level workers start out as technical trainees. At first, trainees perform simple tasks such as marking or blocking the lenses for grinding. As they gain experience and become familiar with the laboratory and the processes, they progress to operations such as lens grinding, lens cutting, edging, beveling, and eyeglass assembly. When trainees have acquired experience in all the principal phases of the work, they are considered all-around technicians. This usually takes six to eight months depending on the learner's aptitude. Some technicians become proficient in only one phase of the operation, such as lens grinding. Learning a single skill takes less time than training to become an all-around technician. Some ophthalmic technicians learn their trade in the armed forces. Others attend one of the small number of formal programs in optical technology offered by vocational-technical or trade schools. To be accredited by the COA these programs must include at least the following:

### Profession-Related Courses
Environmental protection procedures
Fabrication techniques
Frame materials and specifications
Inventory control
Laboratory management
Lens applications
Ophthalmic lens design and types
Ophthalmic medical terminology
Optical theory
Prescription interpretation
Production and quality control
Professional ethics

Relationships with eye care professionals
Surfacing techniques

***General Education Content Areas***
Behavioral science
Communications (oral and written)
Computers
Humanities
Mathematics
Science

Formal programs vary in length from six months to one year. Graduates earn certificates or diplomas.

Ophthalmic technicians who work in larger laboratories can become supervisors and managers. Some technicians become dispensing opticians after completing the additional training that is required.

## Board Certification and Licensure

Opticians must pass the National Opticianry Competency Examination to practice in one of the twenty-six states that require licensing. The American Board of Opticianry (ABO) developed the exam. The written examination consists of three parts: analyzing and interpreting prescriptions, fitting and dispensing spectacles and other ophthalmic devices, and use of standard ophthalmic equipment. Anyone who is at least eighteen years of age and has a high school diploma is eligible to sit for the boards. However, graduates of optical schools or those who have worked in the field for several years are more likely to pass. The exam is intended to test whether an optician is ready for practice. About thirty thousand opticians currently are certified by the ABO, which is about half of those in the profession.

Approximately eight thousand of these opticians are certified by the National Contact Lens Examiners (NCLE). This organization administers the National Contact Lens Registry (NCLR) exam, which consists of four parts: prefit, preparation, and evaluation of contact lens patients; determining lens type and designing contact lens parameters; patient/customer instruction and delivery procedures; and follow-up visits with patients/customers. States that license opticians as contact lens dispensers also require passing scores on this examination.

Both exams are given twice a year. Certification is valid for three years. To be recertified, the optician must submit documentation to show that he or she has participated in the required amount of continuing education.

Licensure for opticians is similar to that of other health professionals. Applicants must submit an application that gives the details of their education, training, and experience. Licenses must be renewed periodically and can be revoked if an optician is found to be incompetent or has been found guilty of improper conduct.

## Compensation and Employment Outlook

There are about sixty-eight thousand dispensing opticians and about thirty-two thousand laboratory technicians working in the United States today. The average earnings of an experienced dispensing optician are estimated at between $19,200 to $31,770 per year. Those working in the offices of ophthalmologists earned the highest salaries; salaries earned in department stores were lower. For ophthalmic laboratory technicians, the average salary was between $17,160 and $25,100. The highest salaries were in manufacturing settings, with lowest earnings in retail stores.

Some positive factors affecting the demand for opticians are the increasing need for eyewear by an aging population, an increase in people's expendable income and interest in fashionable eyewear, and newer technologies, such as progressive lenses and contact lenses to correct presbyopia, which appeal to a large number of baby boomers. The role of the dispensing optician will only expand in this growing marketplace, and opportunities in this profession are expected to increase at least as much as in other fields. For ophthalmic laboratory technicians, the outlook is not as promising. Automation and cheaper foreign manufacturers will reduce the demand for technicians. Most of the need for new workers will come from openings created by retirees or those transferring to other careers.

# 6

# OPHTHALMIC NURSES

OPHTHALMIC NURSES ARE registered nurses who have advanced training in caring for ophthalmology patients. The need for these highly skilled and very versatile nurses has increased dramatically with the growth of outpatient eye surgery centers. Patients are rarely hospitalized now for operations that have become routine outpatient procedures, such as cataract extractions. Ophthalmologists have found that ophthalmic nurses are invaluable both inside and outside the operating room. And nurses have found a new and exciting career path.

## Career Description

This career path starts with basic registered nursing training. Some nurses decide to specialize in eye care when they encounter eye patients in the hospital, where they are being treated for eye trauma or serious diseases that affect their vision. The versatility of ophthalmic nursing appeals to others. Opportunities are available for nurses who like the operating room or office practice or even home care or a combination of these settings. Their duties are varied and it's a job description that is still developing. Ophthalmic nursing is a small, emerging profession, so people who have chosen this career path must be assertive and often must create their own jobs by convincing ophthalmologists that nurses can be an asset in the outpatient setting. An ophthalmic nurse is a change agent who can act as a catalyst for safer and more efficient patient care but who must also be a good team player and work with the existing eye care team in a cohesive manner.

Typical duties for the ophthalmic registered nurse include:

- Performing a detailed and comprehensive nursing assessment of the patient
- Assessing a patient for eye problems using specialized ophthalmic procedures such as direct or indirect ophthalmoloscopy, slit lamp biomicroscopy, IV fluorescein angiography, or ophthalmic ultrasound
- Assisting with contact lens fitting
- Providing health counseling and patient education
- Preparing the patient for surgery
- Assisting the surgeon in the operating room
- Attending the patient after the procedure
- Improving processes to maximize patient safety, risk management, and cost effectiveness

In the eye hospital or ophthalmology department of a general hospital, the ophthalmic nurse may take on other roles. Some ophthalmic nurses have become very skilled physician extenders in the operating room and sometimes function as certified nursing-first assistants, wherein they provide hemostasis, handle tissue, use instruments, and suture the wound. As reimbursement for ophthalmic procedures continues to recede, the demand for nonphysician surgical assistants such as these is expected to increase dramatically. Since operating nurses are a scarce commodity today, nurses in this subspecialty will have their choice of employment situations. The move toward eye surgicenters makes working close to home on a regular daytime schedule a viable option for ophthalmic nurses.

Another nursing specialty that requires advanced training is that of the certified registered nurse anesthetist (CRNA). These nurses care for patients before, during, and after surgery when anesthesia is used. They are experts at monitoring the patient's vital signs and using anesthesia techniques and equipment to ensure the safety and comfort of the patient. The twenty-four-month training program is available to nurses who have attained their bachelor's degree, and it incorporates formal training at the master's level with extensive clinical experiences. CRNAs work under the direction of ophthalmologic surgeons with or without a supervising anesthesiologist, depending on state nursing regulations, in surgicenters, in hospital operating rooms, and in research settings.

## Practice Settings

Ophthalmic nurses work in comfortable environments and generally enjoy better work schedules than do others in the nursing profession. Some of the places where ophthalmic nurses find employment include:

- Ambulatory eye surgery centers
- University or community hospitals with ophthalmology departments

- Ophthalmologists' offices or outpatient clinics
- Home health services
- Ophthalmic research centers
- Eye banks
- Nursing schools and nursing departments' continuing education divisions
- Schools and public health clinics
- Occupational health consultants for businesses
- Case review divisions of insurance providers

Most ophthalmic nurses who are employed in clinical settings work close to home during regular business hours. Hospital nurses may work shifts and some nurses are on-call.

Ophthalmic nurses must have the physical stamina to stand for long periods of time during surgical sessions and must have the emotional fortitude to deal with patients facing disabling illnesses and all sorts of emergencies. Unlike oncology or many other medical specialties, there is very little mortality in ophthalmology, making relationships with patients and their families a positive experience for nurses.

Most nurses are well aware of the hazards of their jobs and have been trained to follow strict guidelines to avoid such dangers as infectious diseases; injuries caused by electrical shocks, chemicals, radiation, or sharp instruments; and strains caused by lifting patients or equipment.

## Education and Training

Ophthalmic nurses complete a regular course of study leading to the registered nurse degree. Their specialized education can be accomplished in several ways. There is a home study course, which is offered by the American Society of Ophthalmic Registered Nurses (ASORN), that is designed to prepare nurses for the certification examination. ASORN also publishes a quarterly journal entitled *Insight*, which includes timely articles of interest to practicing ophthalmic nurses. This organization also distributes other publications about ophthalmic nursing practice including the standards adopted by the American Nursing Association in 1998 for ophthalmic clinical nursing.

Some ophthalmologists prefer to hire registered nurses who have some experience with eye patients, but who are not yet certified. Their training takes place on the job. Using ASORN's publication *Core Curriculum for Ophthalmic Nursing* as a guideline, they are able to prepare for certification while they work in their intended field.

Ophthalmic nurses can also attend seminars sponsored by ASORN and its local and regional chapters. These meeting are accredited for continuing education and offer the opportunity to network with other ophthalmic nurses, peers, and experts to further enhance one's career development.

## Board Certification and Licensure

Ophthalmic nurses must be licensed as registered nurses according to the requirements of the state in which they practice. This generally requires graduating from an accredited nursing school and passing the state's licensing examination.

The National Certifying Board for Ophthalmic Registered Nurses develops and administers the examination that tests the competence of nurses in this field. According to the board, the purpose of the certifying process is to promote the delivery of safe and effective care in ophthalmic registered nursing practice through the certification of qualified ophthalmic registered nurses by:

- Recognizing formally those individuals who meet the eligibility requirements of the National Certifying Board for Ophthalmic Registered Nurses and pass the Certification Examination for Ophthalmic Registered Nurses
- Encouraging continued personal and professional growth in the practice of ophthalmic registered nursing
- Establishing and measuring the level of knowledge required for certification in ophthalmic registered nursing
- Providing a standard of requisite knowledge required for certification, thereby assisting the employer, public, and members of the health professions in the assessment of the ophthalmic registered nurse

Candidates who meet the following criteria are eligible to take the Certification Examination for Ophthalmic Registered Nurses:

- Are currently licensed as registered nurses in the United States or the equivalent in other countries
- Have at least two years of full-time or the equivalent (four thousand hours) experience in ophthalmic registered nursing practice
- Have completed and filed an Application for the Certification Examination for Ophthalmic Registered Nurses
- Have paid the required fee

The exam is given twice a year and costs about $275. It has five sections: Ocular Conditions, Pharmacology, Ophthalmic Nursing

Interventions, Professional Issues, and Nursing Assessment of Ophthalmic Patient.

## Compensation and Employment Outlook

Since there is a relatively small pool of ophthalmic nurses, salary surveys are difficult to find. According to the U.S. Bureau of Labor, the average salary for an experienced registered nurse is about $43,500. For very skilled ophthalmic nurses who assist in the operating room, the salaries are competitive with operating room nurses, who earn between $35,700 as a scrub or circulating nurse and $53,700 as a nursing-first assistant. Because of the shortage of hospital nurses, salaries are increasing more rapidly than for other health professions and probably will continue to do so for nurses who choose to specialize in areas such as ophthalmology.

One of the most interesting factors affecting the demand for nurses has to do with the comfort level of patients. Patients perceive nurses as being extremely well trained and competent, yet compassionate, and this perception makes them a trusted professional in the health care field. Patients may not be familiar with the titles and roles of other ophthalmic workers, but they know about nurses, which makes them valuable additions to the ophthalmology team.

Perhaps the best reason for increasing the use of nurses in ophthalmology has to do with their efficiency. They can perform most of the functions of the ophthalmology office, and they are familiar with how to provide patient care safely and economically.

# 7

---

# OPHTHALMIC AND OPTOMETRIC ASSISTANTS, TECHNICIANS, AND TECHNOLOGISTS

IN EVERY EYE care facility there are a number of highly skilled medical personnel who are qualified by academic and clinical training to provide the support functions of the office or clinic and who perform diagnostic and therapeutic procedures under the direction of an ophthalmologist or optometrist. As a group, these jobs are referred to as *allied medical personnel*. For the purposes of this chapter, they will be referred to as *allied ophthalmic/optometric personnel*. Generally they are classified in three levels. The entry or first level is *assistant*, the intermediate level is *technician*, and the advanced level is *technologist*. In ophthalmology there is also a special certification for *surgical assistants*. The ophthalmic technologist's duties are very similar to those of the ophthalmic registered nurse, although their education and training are very different. Allied ophthalmic/optometric personnel are certified by professional associations, but they are not licensed as independent practitioners. Most work in the private offices of ophthalmologists or optometrists or in hospital clinics. They contribute to the treatment team by providing important information for the diagnosis and treatment plan that is formulated by the supervising eye doctor, but they do not diagnose or prescribe medications for patients.

In optometry, the support staff members are often referred to as *paraoptometric personnel,* and they are certified by the American Optical Association (AOA) in three classifications: certified paraoptometric (CPO), certified paraoptometric assistant (CPOA), and certified paraoptometric technician (CPOT). The CPO certification can be obtained after high school graduation and six months of mentoring by a peer. No formal education is required. The duties and training of the paraoptometric assistants and technicians parallels that of their ophthalmic counterparts in many ways.

Although the functions performed by allied ophthalmic/optometric personnel have always existed, the formal definition and recognition of their jobs as "professions" is a relatively recent development. In 1969 the Joint Committee on Allied Health Personnel in Ophthalmology (JCAHPO) was formed to recognize allied ophthalmic/optometric personnel and develop standards for their training. In 1974 the Council on Health Manpower of the American Medical Association accredited training programs for a single level of expertise: ophthalmic assistants. In 1988 this concept was abandoned in favor of the current three-tier certification program.

## Career Descriptions

The size of the staff and patient load for an eye doctor's practice often determines the responsibilities assigned to support staff. In large practices, assistants typically assume office administrative duties, although a technician in a smaller office might perform these responsibilities. These tasks might include:

- Schedule appointments and greet patients
- Obtain patient data, including patient's self-reported medical history forms; insurance information; medical records and reports from referring physicians, laboratories, and hospitals; and so forth
- Manage and maintain medical records and other files, whether paper or computerized
- Transcribe medical dictation and perform other word processing duties
- Handle telephone calls, correspondence, reports, and manuscripts
- Manage the maintenance functions of the facility
- Maintain and update financial records, including insurance matters, office accounts, collections, payroll, and so forth

Technicians and technologists may perform some or all the following tasks under the supervision of an ophthalmologist or optometrist:

- Collect patient history and physical data
- Administer treatments ordered by the ophthalmologist
- Make anatomical and functional ocular measurements
- Test for ocular function, visual acuity, visual fields, and sensory motor functions
- Administer topical ophthalmic medications
- Instruct patients in the use of contact lenses or self-care requirements
- Assist in fitting contact lenses or eyeglasses

- Make repairs or adjustments to glasses
- Maintain ophthalmic and surgical equipment
- Assist in ophthalmic surgery in the office or hospital

Ophthalmic technologists have the highest level of expertise among the physician extenders. In addition to the tasks listed above, they may also:

- Perform ophthalmic clinical photography
- Perform fluorescent angiography
- Test for ocular motility
- Perform binocular function tests
- Perform microbiological and electrophysiological procedures
- Provide instruction and supervision of personnel
- Conduct patient education sessions

Ophthalmic surgical assistants have special knowledge and skills in the following areas:

- Preoperative preparation of patients
- Surgical instruments
- Aseptic technique
- Ophthalmic anesthesia
- Ophthalmic surgical procedures
- Surgical complications
- Ophthalmic surgical pharmacology
- Minor surgery

Whatever the level, allied ophthalmic/optometric personnel make a major contribution to the productivity of the office and the quality of care afforded to its patients. Effective support staffs know how to work efficiently while being friendly, calm, and unhurried. They learn how to be good listeners and are often able to glean helpful information for the ophthalmologist or optometrist just by chatting with a patient.

## Practice Settings

As in the other eye care professions, allied ophthalmic/optometric personnel work in pleasant surroundings. Offices are clean, comfortable, and attractive. Although workers are expected to be productive, there is usually a close relationship between the eye doctor and his or her support team.

Since eye care facilities can be found in almost any community, employment close to home is generally a good possibility. The higher salaries and more specialized positions are found in metropolitan areas in practices associated with, or employed by, hospitals and medical schools.

Most allied ophthalmic/optometric personnel work in the private offices of eye doctors, but they are also employed in these settings:

- Private group practice
- Private solo practice
- Multispecialty clinic
- Hospital
- University clinic
- HMO/PPO
- Consultant/self-employed
- Ophthalmic instrument manufacturer
- Ophthalmic pharmaceutical sales
- Public health clinic

The work is not physically demanding, but it is somewhat stressful in busy offices. This is a career for the "people person," and only those who are tolerant of people suffering from illness should pursue it. Since many patients are older people, this is a career for those who enjoy working with this population.

Most eye doctors now have evening and weekend appointments to accommodate working patients. Depending on the size of the staff, support personnel are expected to share night and weekend duties. Since surgery is usually scheduled during the day on a fixed schedule, ophthalmic technologists usually have a weekday routine, unless the office takes emergency cases. Then the technologists may need to be on-call.

Most allied ophthalmic/optometric personnel work full-time. Flexible scheduling is becoming more popular as the competition for good workers increases. About 90 percent of the workforce is made up of women; this is a career that blends well with family life.

## Education and Training

Perhaps one of the best features of this career choice is the flexibility that the Joint Commission on Allied Health Personnel in Ophthalmology allows in attaining the requirements for the various skill levels. There are many accredited training programs in the United States and Canada for ophthalmic personnel. The prerequisite for all programs is a high school diploma or its equivalent. Programs of study that are accredited by the Committee on Accreditation for Ophthalmic Medical Personnel, in cooperation with the Commission on Accreditation of Allied Health Educational Programs, are sponsored by colleges, universities, medical schools, and other institutions. The course of study can last from four to twelve months for assistants, and there are two-year programs for technicians and technologists. There are other routes to certification that include work experience plus a home-study course, and approved continuing education "short courses." For those who want to pursue a college degree, certification has the equivalence of college credits. The certified ophthalmic assistant exam carries twelve college credits, the certified ophthalmic technician exam sixteen college credits, and the certified ophthalmic medical technologist exam eighteen college credits. Course work usually includes:

Anatomy and physiology—basic and ocular
Medical terminology
Medical law and ethics
Psychology
Ophthalmic optics
Microbiology
Ophthalmic pharmacology and toxicology
Ocular motility
Diseases of the eye
Diagnostic and treatment procedures
Visual field testing
Contact lenses
Ophthalmic surgery
Proper care and maintenance of ophthalmic equipment and
    instruments

These courses plus supervised, clinical, hands-on training are directed at preparing the student for the certification examination as well as the world of work.

Since an ophthalmologist's endorsement is required for certification, almost all applicants have worked in that setting. Some start as receptionists and return to their sponsor's office. Others go on to run laboratories in hospitals or work on research projects at university medical schools or pharmaceutical companies. Some go on to teach in preparation programs.

Optometric assistants and technicians also have flexibility in how they meet the educational requirements for their professions. There are accredited programs at community colleges, universities, and trade schools, or one can choose a self-study course. Some schools offer distance learning or course work online over the Internet, with the addition of on-site tutoring for hands-on training. The course work is similar to the ophthalmic counterpart, but there is more emphasis placed on the subjects of optics, dispensing, and refraction since this is a large part of the optometrist's job. Paraoptometric students learn about the anatomy and physiology of the eye, the mechanics of vision, and symptoms of eye disorders. By the end of their training, they are experts at selecting, fitting, and repairing lenses, frames, and contact lenses.

## Board Certification and Licensure

The Joint Commission on Allied Health Personnel in Ophthalmology has been certifying ophthalmic support staffs since 1969. Certification is available at three levels and for one subspecialty. Certified ophthalmic assistant (COA) is the entry level, certified ophthalmic technician (COT) is the middle level, and certified ophthalmic medical technologist (COMT) is the highest level. Individuals who are already certified at one of the three "core" levels can go on for a subspecialty certification in ophthalmic surgical assisting.

The written part of the examination for ophthalmic staff is computerized. The results of the test are available as soon as it is completed. The written test is intended to evaluate a candidate's mastery of the course work and knowledge needed to perform the duties listed earlier in this chapter. There is also a practical, hands-on exam for COT and COMT. The performance exam tests the ability to perform patient examinations and the clinical procedures that are part of the job. The written test is given periodically at various locations throughout the country. The performance exam is offered twice a year.

Once certification is obtained, the JCAHPO requires that all levels of personnel complete continuing education requirements. In a field that changes as quickly as ophthalmology, continuing education is necessary to provide state-of-the-art care for patients.

Certification for optometric assistants and technicians is similar. There is a written exam for both levels and a practical exam for technicians. The American Optometric Association administers the certification process. Recertification is required every three years. A minimum of sixteen continuing education credits is required. A list of acceptable education sponsors and subject matter is available from the AOA.

At this time there are no licensing requirements for optometric/ophthalmic assistants in any states. Some states do have licensing requirements for ophthalmic/optometric technicians and technologists, particularly if they are involved in the dispensing of eyewear. There are also some state regulations for ophthalmologists and optometrists concerning the supervision of technicians and technologists.

## Compensation and Employment Outlook

Salaries for ophthalmic/optometric assistants, technicians, and technologists have increased significantly over the last few years. There is a wide range of salaries, between $20,000 and $60,000 per year based on the skill level. In general, assistants can expect to earn in the mid- to upper twenties, and technologists command a higher salary of about $50,000. Pay scales vary according to the geographic location and practice size and type.

Employment for all levels of ophthalmic/optometric allied personnel is expected to be much better than average through the year 2010. A major factor affecting the need is the increase in outpatient offices and clinics. The cost-effectiveness of using paraprofessionals will make these jobs in great demand. Job candidates with certification will be the most sought after. As ophthalmologists and optometrists experience a continued decline in reimbursement for services, they will need to increase their productivity by using more office staff to see more patients. Using paraprofessionals will allow them to provide quality care at a lower cost than will sharing income with another physician. The anticipated demand for these workers will far exceed the supply. Competition for certified, experienced workers will compel employers to offer flexible scheduling, higher compensation, and excellent benefits packages as recruitment incentives.

# 8

## Related Occupations

In addition to the clinical careers that form the core of patient services in the field of eye care, there are many opportunities for people in support roles. These careerists often have training that would qualify them for positions in other branches of health care or in other industries. Their particular interest in being part of the eye care team motivated them to seek additional training and specialization. Many of these specialized jobs have become such an integral part of the provision of vision services that professional associations have formed to certify those who meet credentialing requirements. Just a few of these careers are described in this chapter.

## Ophthalmic Photographers

Ophthalmic photography is one of the largest specialties within the new and growing field of medical photography and illustration. On the surface, the ophthalmic photographer's role seems simple; he or she provides a visual record of the eye and its parts. In actuality, the exacting science of capturing subtle changes that help in tracking diseases and isolating eye functions for study and research makes ophthalmic photography an invaluable tool.

Since ophthalmic photographers must combine their artistic talent with technical knowledge of the anatomy and physiology of the eye, new entrants in this field seem to come from two areas. Many are people who have studied photography in college and worked as news, magazine, or commercial photographers. Some have completed degrees in medical illustration, with photography as their preferred medium. On the other end of the spectrum are ophthalmic technicians, who may have been amateur photographers and developed skills that have led to a new direction in their careers.

Ophthalmic photography has become such an important part of eye care that certification of photographers is now available and desired by potential employers. To become a Certified Retinal Angiographer (CRA), the photographer must present a portfolio of his or her work and pass both written and oral examinations administered by the Ophthalmic Photographers Society. The society serves not only as the certifying body for photographers but also offers educational seminars, publishes the *Journal of Ophthalmic Photography*, and organizes conferences and networking opportunities for its members. Recertification is required every three years, and CRAs must show that they have taken continuing education courses to keep up with the changing technologies of photography and eye care. Longtime members who have contributed to the field are eligible to become fellows of the society.

Ophthalmic photographers generally work for eye institutes or large hospitals where there are research and educational programs.

They perform a wide range of functions—from teaching technologists how to do fundus photography, flourescein angiography, and slit lamp to videotaping surgical procedures in the operating room. Some of their work is used to illustrate articles in ophthalmic journals or for slide presentations at medical conferences. Since this is a new and very high-tech field, experienced photographers sometimes get the opportunity to apply new technologies such as electronic digitized imaging. There are also opportunities to do consulting work on research projects and with manufacturers to develop new products.

## Ophthalmic Administrators

Ophthalmic administrators generally have a master's degree in health administration. In addition to their preparation to become health care business managers, they also must learn the particulars of ophthalmic clinical practice. Ophthalmic administrators are experts on the volatile marketplace and ever-changing world of government regulations. Administrators have a wide range of responsibilities, including managing the day-to-day operation of a facility; planning new programs and practice sites; monitoring budgets, billing, collections, and personnel matters; recruiting new doctors and staff; fund-raising; marketing; and a host of other functions.

Administrators often report to both a physician director and administrative director. In an academic setting, the ophthalmology department may be a small division in a large institution. Administrators have to be diplomatic and astute at protecting their division's resources within the framework of a larger organization. Successful administrators are problem solvers who can bring good conceptual and analytic thinking together with effective interpersonal skills. They can go on to become a top administrator at a larger health care facility.

Many of these professionals belong to the American Society of Ophthalmic Administrators (ASOA), which now offers the certified ophthalmic administrator credential after the applicant passes a three-hour board certification exam. The ASOA sponsors a website where administrators can get information about continuing education and employment opportunities.

## Researchers

Researchers are often tucked away in remote laboratories of eye institutes working on cutting-edge treatments or advancing knowledge about the functions of the visual system. Most researchers have Ph.D. degrees in a scientific field such as biology, chemistry, or physics; some are medical doctors as well, and they work in tandem with other clinical and teaching physicians. Their work is very exacting and requires patience and a curiosity that transcends the sometimes repetitious laboratory routines and paperwork that are part of scientific research.

A researcher's income is often variable since he or she is dependent on grant support from government agencies, like the National Eye Institute, or private and corporate foundations. Ophthalmologists who teach are also frequently involved in research. Ophthalmic researchers can hold salaried positions with companies that manufacture pharmaceuticals or medical equipment.

Researchers who work for medical or pharmaceutical companies are usually involved in the development of new products. The U.S. Food and Drug Administration has very stringent regulations about the testing of new drugs and devices in order to protect patients.

Many researchers are specialists in designing and monitoring "clinical trials," in which hospital patients or human volunteers use a new product in the final testing stages.

## Vision Science Librarians

In this daunting age of information, particularly with easier access to the Internet, busy eye care professionals need an expert to help them find just what they need to know—whether it is an exhaustive or very focused search. In the eye care world, it is the vision science librarian who provides this invaluable service to ophthalmologists, optometrists, allied health professionals, students in eye care training programs, researchers, administrators, patients, and anyone else who needs to know about the eye and vision. Many of the libraries and media centers where they work are based in eye hospitals, ophthalmology departments of university medical schools, optometric colleges, or private companies with an interest in vision-related products and services.

Vision science librarians provide reference materials, computerized literature searches, audiovisual services, interlibrary loan document delivery, and other library services to the staff of their institutions. These librarians, who are a specialized type of medical librarian, often offer consumer health information about eye care to the general public and provide patient education materials for visually impaired persons and their families.

Most vision science librarians have master's degrees in library or information science. They sometimes have undergraduate degrees in biology or another scientific discipline. An interest in computerized information databases and, today, the Internet are now an essential part of the job. Much of the information that is needed by health care professionals is found in periodical literature that can be located by searching online indexes. Some vision science librarians also have developed their own internal data banks for quick retrieval of in-house information. Librarians who work in this type of environment generally develop close ties with the researchers, students, faculty, and practitioners who are frequent clients. Unlike others in academic or public library settings, the vision science librarian has the satisfaction of seeing or hearing about the results of his or her information support services.

Many of these librarians are members of the Association for Vision Science Librarians (AVSL) and the Medical Library Association (MLA). AVSL maintains a website with interesting information about eye care including a list of statistics. MLA offers continuing education opportunities for librarians working in health care settings and has a fellowship program that is similar to certification.

# 9

# Trying an Eye Care Career
# on for Size

Now THAT YOU have read the descriptions of various eye care careers, perhaps you have an idea of which one is for you. Since most eye care careers require several years of education and training, it is a good idea to find out if you are well suited for the field before making the time and financial commitments. Here are several ways to get started on the career path in eye care that is exactly right for you.

## Volunteer Work

Volunteerism is in! But it has changed dramatically since the women who made up the traditional pool of helpers found paying jobs. Contemporary volunteers are all ages, come from various walks of life, and donate their time for a variety of reasons. Many retirees do volunteer work to stay active. People new to a community often donate their nonworking hours to learn more about their new community and meet people. Volunteering is also a good way to explore new or second career options. Most of the volunteers who work in hospitals or for other health services agencies will tell you that there is great satisfaction in knowing that the services they provide help patients.

Volunteer opportunities in eye care are abundant. The important thing to remember is to find a volunteer position that provides you with an opportunity to experience the career setting in which you would like to work. Your expectations about this "precareer" experience should be discussed with the volunteer coordinator before you sign on, so that both your needs and those of the institution are met.

If you are undecided about which career option is for you, volunteer work in a hospital or eye institute will give you the exposure to workers, patients, and other elements of the eye care environment that you need to make a decision. You should contact the volunteer services coordinator at a local eye institute or hospital that is affiliated with a medical school teaching program. In addition to working with inpatient services, you might have a chance to observe community outreach programs, such as mobile vision-screening vans or satellite clinics in nursing home and neighborhood health centers.

The perception that hospital volunteers roll bandages and do menial work is outdated. Today's hospitals are short on staff in so many areas that your assignment could be one of your choosing and can be matched to your special talents and interests. Hospital volunteers are needed to escort and visit patients, help out in offices, do research in the medical library, program computers, run audiovisual equipment for educational conferences, prepare public relations packets, manage the gift shop, organize fund-raisers, or do almost any job that does not require clinical licensing. In many ways, volunteers provide the extra level of caring and excellence that makes a hospital better.

## Community Agencies

If your goal for volunteer work is to work with many patients or a specific type of visual disability, community agencies are a good source for this type of experience. Most states, counties, and large municipalities have an association for the blind and visually impaired that includes an information and referral service that lists volunteer needs. Community agencies that serve this population generally offer the following services:

- Counseling of individuals and families
- Free/low cost transportation to medical facilities, shopping, and recreational activities
- Health equipment loans or consumer advice about equipment (talking-book machines, canes, radios, glasses, and so forth)
- Vision screening and education for the community
- Job placement and development
- Recreation (luncheons, parties, games, meetings, and so on)
- Rehabilitation outpatient care (Braille instruction, use of household appliances, instruction in independent travel, adapted work or study skills, and other types of care services)
- Recruitment of readers and recorders

You can locate these agencies by looking in the yellow pages of the telephone book or by asking for a directory of community service groups at your local public library.

The key to a successful and fulfilling volunteer experience is matching your goals with those of the institution or agency. If you want to observe ophthalmic technicians on the job, let the volunteer coordinator know, or you may end up in the linen room!

## Part-Time Jobs

Many eye care professionals own their own businesses. A good way to learn about this side of eye care is to start at the bottom and work your way up. Part-time jobs are a good way to gain some insight on the marketplace aspects of health care. Part-time employment may be educational and help to pay some bills, but it might not be glamorous. Many part-timers do paperwork in doctors' offices or stock shelves in stores. The object is not to get rich, but to watch your boss so that you can gain an understanding of the rewards and responsibilities of self-employment. Your boss, of course, will provide more guidance if he or she knows this is your intention. Ophthalmologists and optometrists often act as sponsors or references for employees who would like to enter technical or business training programs.

Part-time jobs are getting more plentiful and are frequently advertised in the employment section of the newspaper. One of the best ways to find a job in eye care is to use networking. You can do this by spreading the word among your friends, teachers, acquaintances, and relatives that you are interested in eye care–related employment opportunities. If you know someone whose parent or friend is an optometrist, ask to meet that person to discuss your career exploration plan. Ask the optometrist to keep you in mind for any job openings he or she hears about.

A one-page résumé is a good tool for communicating your skills and plans to prospective employers. Review the sections in this book on the eye care careers that interest you. Then use your résumé to summarize the relevant skills and education you have acquired in preparation for an eye care career. Remember to update your résumé as you take on additional responsibilities in your new part-time job. Dealing with customers, developing marketing ideas, coding insurance forms, and updating patient education materials are the types of skills that will show schools and full-time employers that you are committed to professional growth and a good candidate for advanced training or promotion.

## Internships

Internships are generally educational experiences that are designed to give the participant exposure to a future career. Summer internships are becoming more popular with nonprofit organizations that need help but have limited funding. For you, an internship is an excellent opportunity to try a career, because instead of pay, you can structure an educational experience that might expose you to more situations than would a part-time or volunteer job. Many organizations use interns to help with special projects that they do not have staff or time to accomplish. As part of the educational experience, you probably will be required to write a paper, do a presentation, or complete an assigned project. Your high school or college also may grant academic credit for your internship, if it is approved ahead of time. You can locate internships by contacting the career counseling office at your school or by calling one of the service organizations listed in Appendix A of this book or some other organization where you would like to work. If the organization does not have an internship program, ask to meet with a staff member who needs help with a special project and submit a proposal for an educational experience that would help both you and your mentor. Who could resist a go-getter intern like that?

Don't forget to keep a record of exactly what you do as a volunteer or part-timer. This experience will form the basis of a résumé that you can use for later jobs. It will show your early commitment to your chosen career. Make sure that you keep up-to-date information about people you work with and who can provide references.

## Find a Mentor

A quick and easy way to vicariously explore an eye care career—aside from reading about one—is to interview someone who is already in the job that interests you. Most health care careerists are in their chosen "helping" profession because they like people and find their work very rewarding. They are generally flattered to be asked to describe their career accomplishments.

Once you have found a likely role model—you might ask your guidance counselor to help with this—be sure you have prepared a list of questions that covers all of your concerns about your prospective career choice. It is a good idea to have some "ice breaker" topics to discuss first. Here are some possible questions:

- Why did you choose optometry?
- What are the positive and negative aspects of your job?
- Would you want your son or daughter to follow in your footsteps? Why?

If you feel that you and your mentor are comfortable with each other, you should ask more personal questions, like:

- How do you balance a career in ophthalmology with family life?
- What was the most difficult part of starting your optometry business?

Learning from those who are more experienced in your intended field is what the mentoring process is all about. This is an effective method for acquiring personalized guidance to help you advance and succeed in your eye care career.

## Virtual Eye Care Careers: Surfing the Internet

In the appendixes of this book there are references to Internet websites. If you are not computer-literate or have never used the Internet, it is time to explore this exciting resource. You can get the training you need at school or at your local library. Larger public libraries frequently have computers where you can learn and use the Internet.

Once you know how to access the Internet, you will find that typing keywords that describe your area of interest into your search software will connect you with some of the most interesting sites that contain many screens of information, including color photographs. This information can be downloaded onto your personal computer and then printed. One of the marvels of the Internet is its unique ability to be interactive in real time. It's the next best thing to being there!

Other ways of experiencing the world of eye care professionals before you take the plunge is to read what they read. You can use the Internet to peruse the full text of many professional and scientific periodicals and documents without traveling to a university library. Many of the training programs listed in Appendix C provide information about their curricula on their Web pages. The professional organizations listed in Appendix A often provide credentialing or certification standards that are considered state-of-the-art skills for the profession you are interested in pursuing. You also can review the credentials and interests of faculty members who might become your role models. Sometimes it is possible to access their students' homework assignments or review their reading materials to get an idea of the scope and difficulty of a particular course.

And when you are ready to look for that full-time job, posting your résumé online is a popular way to job hunt these days. You can compare your experience and plans with those of young professionals who are upwardly mobile.

Since Internet addresses change a lot, some of the resources suggested here may not be accessible by the time you get to try them, and as soon as this book is in print, there will be a host of new websites. It's hard to keep up, so the best advice is to learn to use a Web browser or search engine so that you can select from everything that is available when you need it. You'll find a list of favorite websites for general information on eye care and related careers in Appendix B. Explore these and make your own list of favorites.

# 10

---

# What Everyone Should Know About Healthy Eyes and Good Vision

THERE IS AN old saying that goes, "Our eyes are our windows on the world." This means that almost everything we do or think about is influenced by what we see. If you have ever been blindfolded, you know how losing your sight for even a few minutes can be frightening and confusing. Think for a moment about what life would be like if you were to lose your eyesight permanently. You would miss the colors of fall trees, and you could not experience the shock of a horror movie; it would be hard to know what your friends were really thinking without seeing their faces. You would not be able to read this book or go to work or school without the aid of special equipment. Unfortunately, almost everyone has to face some degree of vision loss as part of the aging process. So it is important to learn everything—whether you become an eye care professional or not—about how to maintain your good vision for as long as you can and to be well informed about the warning signs and options for treatment of vision-threatening conditions.

In eye care, as in other health care fields, there are professionals who specialize in the study and treatment of one disease, like glaucoma or strabismus, and there are those who limit their practice to one part of the eye, such as the retina. To the layperson, these words may be as difficult to say, spell, and pronounce as is a foreign language. For the practicing eye care specialist, medical terminology is a communication tool that is universally understood by others in the field.

Medical terminology should not be a foreign language to anyone. It is the language that well-informed health care consumers should master so that they can converse with their care providers. Everyone can benefit from taking the time to learn more about the technical aspects of visual health.

Students who are preparing for careers in the ophthalmic sciences learn about the parts of the eye and visual system in anatomy and physiology courses. To adequately care for patients, eye care professionals—regardless of their scope of practice—must have a clear understanding of how the eye functions.

## The Eye

A cone-shaped socket called the orbit surrounds the eye. Fatty tissue lines the orbit, forming a cushion for the eyeball, and six muscles move the eye. These muscles operate much like puppet strings.

The brow, upper and lower eyelids, and eyelashes protect the eyeball from dust and foreign objects. The conjunctiva—a mucous membrane—lines the inside of the eyelids and continues over the forepart of the eyeball. As we blink, mucus and tears from the lacrimal glands are distributed over the eye to keep it moist.

There are three layers of tissue that form the wall of the eyeball. The sclera and cornea form the outside layer. The sclera is the "white of the eye" that covers almost the entire visible eye. The cornea is the transparent shield that enables light rays to enter the eye.

The main part of the middle layer of the wall—or uveal tract— is the colored iris. Whether your eyes are blue, green, hazel, or brown depends on the amount of melanin—a light-absorbing pigment—they have. Blue-eyed people have less of this brownish-black substance than brown-eyed people do. The black disk inside the iris is the pupil, which can be dilated by two muscles when looking at far objects. The ciliary body encircles the iris and serves two functions. It adjusts the lens behind the cornea to create crisp images, and it produces the clear, watery fluid that lubricates the cornea and lens. The back layer of the uveal tract is the choroid, a blood-vessel-laden tissue that nourishes the retina.

The retina is the very fragile interior wall of the eyeball. Light-sensitive retinal cells—called rods and cones—change light into electrical signals. It is the macula at the center of the retina that produces the sharp images that we see while looking directly at an object. The rest of the retina assists with peripheral vision and seeing shades of gray and colors. Nerve fibers join the rods and cones to the optic nerve at the base of the retina. Electrical impulses from the retina are cabled to the brain, which interprets the visual images. Approximately one-third of the brain is involved in the processing of visual signals and information. This activity is conducted constantly during waking hours and continues to some extent during sleep, particularly during the active dreaming periods of sleep.

Most of the interior of the eyeball is filled with the vitreous humor, a clear jellylike mass. Like the air in a basketball, the vitreous humor maintains the shape and pressure within the eyeball.

## How We See

A tiny image of the objects we look at is projected on the retina when light reflected from the object is bent by the cornea and lens. The bending, or refractive power of the eye, aims light at the macula for the sharpest images.

In a process called *accommodation*, the ciliary body compresses the lens to make it thicker for viewing distant objects and stretches it for seeing close up. The eye must constantly change as we focus on different objects, making it impossible to have a clear image of both a close and a distant object at the same time.

## Maintaining Visual Health

Seeing is very much like the telephone system. Vision results from a complicated network of messages that are "communicated" from the eye to the brain. As with the phone system, there are many things, such as aging, injury, or disease, that can cause an interruption in eye-to-brain service. Breakdowns in the visual system can be dealt with in different ways—from prescribing medications to dispensing eyeglasses to doing laser surgery.

The key to maintaining a good visual system is early intervention. If you have any of the signs and symptoms listed below, contact your eye care professional at once:

- Blurry vision uncorrectable by lenses
- Double vision
- Dimming of vision that comes and goes or sudden loss of vision
- Red eye

- Eye pain
- Loss of side vision
- Halos (colored rays or circles around lights)
- Crossed, turned, or wandering eye
- Twitching or shaking eyes
- Flashes or streaks of light
- New floaters (spots, strings, or shadows)
- Discharge, crusting, or excessive tearing of the eye
- Swelling of any part of the eye
- Bulging of one or both eyes
- Difference in size of the eyes
- Drooping eyelids
- Constant squinting
- Sensitivity to light

## Regular Exams

Even if you do not have any symptoms of eye problems, the best way to maintain your vision is to have early detection and treatment of eye problems. The best way to do this is to have regular examinations by a qualified optometrist or ophthalmologist. Since your age and medical history are the determining factors in the frequency of these exams, the American Academy of Ophthalmology recommends the following examination interval guidelines:

- At or before the age of four for children
- Every three to five years if you are age thirty-nine or over
- Every one to two years if you are age fifty or over, if a family member has glaucoma or other inherited disease, or if you have had a serious eye injury in the past

## Prevention and Safety

Even if you have perfect sight, maintaining your vision is as important as any other aspect of your health. Unfortunately our homes, workplaces, and recreational activities are full of hazards that threaten our good sight. Being aware of these hazards is the first step to preventing serious injury or blindness.

Eye care professionals report that each year as many as ten million patients complain of vision problems related to computers and video games. Extended viewing of video monitors is less than ideal and can cause eye fatigue and dryness. Fortunately, taking a few precautions can prevent the scratchy, burning sensation that bothers frequent computer users. Here are a few reminders for comfortable computer use:

- To reduce glare, place the top of the screen at eye level or slightly below or attach a screen filter to your monitor.
- Reduce the strain on your eyes by taking a ten- to fifteen-minute break every few hours to focus on a distant object.
- To prevent dry eyes, make a conscious effort to blink more frequently or ask your pharmacist to recommend lubricating eye drops or "artificial tears."
- Ask your eye care professional if you would benefit from wearing special lenses made especially for computer users.

## Eye Safety for Sports and Recreation

Believe it or not, each year more than one hundred thousand eye injuries occur while we are enjoying sports and recreational activities. Tragically, more than half of these injuries happens to children playing or engaging in sports. Sports- and play-related eye injuries can result in blindness or even cause glaucoma years later. That is why it is important to have your family doctor or an eye care professional check even a minor eye injury.

However, with the proper protective equipment or safety procedures, most of these injuries can be prevented. Contrary to popular belief, shatterproof street-wear glasses and soft contact lenses do not constitute protective eyewear. A discussion of sports-related eye protection should be a part of everyone's annual checkup with an eye care professional.

Here are some guidelines for recreational eye safety:

- For basketball, tennis, soccer, and all racquetball sports, wear prescription or nonprescription polycarbonate sports eye guards with side shields.
- For baseball and lacrosse, wear a helmet a with polycarbonate face mask or wire shield.
- For ice hockey, helmets should be approved by the Hockey Equipment Certification Council (HECC) or the Canadian Standards Association (CSA).
- For skiing, wear goggles or glasses that filter ultraviolet light and excessive sunlight.
- For boxing, there is no adequate eye protection, but thumbless gloves are believed to reduce injuries.

The following precautions should be taken to protect children at play:

- Choose games and toys that are age-appropriate and have an adult supervise play.
- Select toys labeled "ASTM approved," which shows that the product meets the standards set by the American Society for Testing and Materials International.

- Avoid projectile toys (darts, bows and arrows, and so forth) and air-powered guns.
- Keep children away from fireworks and chemicals that can spray into eyes.
- Do not allow children to play in an area where lawn mowers or power tools are in use.

## The Hazards of Exposure to Sunlight

Research has shown that prolonged exposure to the sun can threaten your sight and cause skin problems. The sun's rays produce ultraviolet (UV) light in two wavelengths that are dangerous: UV-A wavelengths contribute to skin aging and UV-B is the type of radiation that causes sunburn and skin cancer. Both types can cause ocular damage, which results in a greater incidence of glaucoma, macular degeneration, and cataracts.

The American Academy of Ophthalmology makes the following recommendations for protecting against overexposure to the sun:

- Always wear appropriate sunscreen, a hat, and sunglasses when out in the sun for extended periods.
- Make sure your sunglasses block 99 or 100 percent of UV rays (check the label).
- If you spend prolonged time in the sun or on the water during the middle of the day, wear close-fitting goggles or sunglasses with lenses that absorb all UV-A and UV-B. Blue light absorption may be helpful as well.
- If you feel you must use a tanning booth, make sure the salon gives you (sterilized) protective eye goggles, as required by the FDA.

# Normal Aging

Even eyes that are well cared for will age like other parts of the body. It is normal for the lens and muscles that control the lens to lose their elasticity, making it harder to focus on objects at close range. *Presbyopia* (aging eyes) affects many middle-aged adults who suddenly find that they can no longer read small print without holding it at arm's length. Fortunately, the days of telltale bifocal-lined glasses are over, and "presbyops" have many attractive options such as blended lenses and contacts.

Unlike many other aspects of aging, presbyopia stabilizes in later life. This occurs at about the same time, in the late sixties and early seventies, when older adults should be particularly vigilant about serious age-related diseases such as cataracts and glaucoma.

Can you prolong your youthful sight by eating wisely? Remember what your mother told you about eating carrots for good eyesight? She was partially right. Carrots are a wonderful source of vitamin A, which does aid in good vision. However, recent research shows that the antioxidants in other foods such as spinach, broccoli, green beans, corn, and peaches may slow cell degeneration in the body, including the eyes. These foods contain compounds known as *carotenoids*, one of which, lutein, has been shown to reduce the incidence of macular degeneration and cataracts. Lutein now appears as a popular ingredient in multivitamin supplements that are formulated especially for mature adults.

# Especially for Women

Although women share many of the same risks to their vision as men, there are several uniquely female aspects of eye care. The first has to do with estrogen, the hormone that regulates a woman's reproductive life. As the levels of estrogen fluctuate during the menstrual cycle, pregnancy, or menopause, some women experience changes in their vision. Symptoms usually include intermittent bouts of blurry vision and discomfort in wearing contact lenses. Fortunately, these symptoms are usually minor, temporary, and treatable in consultation with an eye care professional. More serious problems can sometimes be encountered during pregnancy. Women who develop gestational diabetes are at risk for retinal detachment. Other moms-to-be find that they must discontinue wearing contact lenses or update their prescription for glasses frequently during the term of their pregnancy.

One other risk factor for women is the wearing of makeup. The chemical ingredients in makeup and the bacteria it harbors can be hazardous to eyesight. The following are some guidelines for those who wear makeup:

- For contact lens wearers, use hypoallergenic makeup and oil-free products.
- Avoid using caustic chemicals that might damage plastic lenses, such as nail polish remover or perfume.
- Discard old cosmetics, as they may contain bacteria that might cause eye infections.
- Never use another person's cosmetics to avoid infections or allergic reactions.

## Disorders of the Visual System

Disorders of the eye and visual system are widespread among Americans. Current estimates indicate that as many as four out of every one thousand Americans is legally blind. Almost everyone would agree that losing one's sight would be devastating, but few are familiar with the actual causes of blindness.

In a person with normal vision, several complicated systems function well and in a coordinated fashion. Impaired vision occurs when the system malfunctions because of an inherited abnormality or from aging, injury, or disease. Eye care professionals are trained to precisely diagnose these impairments and to formulate a restorative plan for the patient from a myriad of treatment options. In many cases, early intervention is the key to saving one's sight. Knowing the basics about eye disorders and diseases will give you not only the tools for maintaining your own good vision, but a real appreciation for the expertise that must be developed by eye care professionals as well.

## *Improving Refractive Errors*

Difficulty in focusing or seeing a clear image is called a *refractive error*. These are very common and can be fully corrected with eyeglasses or contact lenses. Some of the refractive errors frequently treated by eye care professionals include:

- **Myopia, or nearsightedness.** Distances are blurred because the eye is longer than normal and the image is focused in front of the retina.
- **Hyperopia, or farsightedness.** Near objects are blurred because the eye is shorter than normal and the image is focused behind the retina.
- **Astigmatism.** Vision is blurred at all distances because the image does not focus in one position on the retina.
- **Presbyopia.** Reading materials and near objects are blurred because the clear lens at the front of the eye gets cloudier as people age.

Refractive errors, frequently myopia, are common in about one in five children in the United States. And as we age, presbyopia affects almost everyone. Currently, about 150 million Americans wear glasses or contact lenses to correct their refractive errors, spending more than $15 billion annually on eyewear. The optics industry is expected to grow as the population ages. This makes it a secure job market for optometrists, opticians, and technicians.

Dramatic advances in the surgical correction of refractive errors have given the patient a dizzying array of options to wearing glasses and contact lenses. Anyone who is considering these alternatives should become well informed about both the ophthalmologist and the surgical procedure that will be performed. Today, surgeons expect their patients to ask them some direct questions. These might include:

- How many procedures have you performed?
- How long have you been performing these procedures?
- What percentage of your patients achieves 20/20 vision or better?
- How often have complications occurred, such as infection, having to perform the operation twice, and other adverse results?
- Have you ever been denied malpractice insurance coverage?
- Is your medical license in good standing?

Being an informed patient means knowing about and discussing with your surgeon the expected positive and negative results of the type of surgery you are anticipating and reviewing the consent form that you will be asked to sign. Don't forget to discuss the cost, the time period for the operation and recuperation, and whether you will need to bring someone with you to drive you home and care for you the day of your procedure. Information about all of the surgeries listed below, including testimonials of patients, is available from the organizations listed in Appendix A. Currently, the following procedures are approved in both the United States and Canada to correct refractive errors:

• Laser Assisted in Keratomileusis (LASIK) is currently the most popular and effective laser procedure for correcting nearsightedness, farsightedness, and astigmatism. The LASIK procedure takes about one minute per eye and involves the use of a keratome (scalpel) and excimer laser to remove a thin layer of tissue from the center of the cornea to flatten it.

• Photorefractive Keratectomy (PRK) also corrects near- and farsightedness and astigmatism. It is often recommended for patients with larger or thinner corneas who are not appropriate candidates for LASIK. When performing PRK, the ophthalmologist uses an excimer laser to flatten the cornea. The procedure has been performed in Canada since 1978 and was approved in the United States in 1995 as safe and effective.

• Radial Keratotomy (RK) is an outpatient surgical procedure that has been used since the 1970s to correct myopia by reshaping the curvature of the cornea with microscopic incisions made by an ophthalmologist in a radial or spokelike pattern around the cornea. This procedure permanently changes the shape of the cornea, resulting in the long-term correction of nearsightedness. This improvement occasionally diminishes with time.

• Astigmatic Keratotomy (AK) is sometimes used in conjunction with RK or other laser procedures to correct astigmatism. The procedure involves surgical incisions made in a curved pattern on the cornea, which is then reshaped into a more normal spherical form.

• Automated Lamellar Keratoplasty (ALK) is a type of surgery where the ophthalmologist cuts a flap of tissue across the cornea. If additional tissue under the flap is removed, high levels of myopia can be corrected. If a thin level of tissue is retained and stretched under the flap, there is a correction for hypermyopia.

### Low Vision

People of all ages can be affected by low vision, which means that their vision cannot be corrected with conventional glasses and contact lenses. Many of these people with low vision can read, play cards, watch television, and in other ways function and enjoy life with the use of special low-vision devices. These include:

- Magnifying spectacles that are stronger than most ordinary glasses
- Hand and stand magnifiers that may also have a light source
- Telescopes for viewing distant items, closed-circuit TV to enlarge images on the screen, and special home and work devices such as enlarged phone dials and clock faces

## Diseases of the Visual System

Perhaps the greatest challenge to the eye care team is the diagnosis and treatment of vision-threatening diseases. Optometrists and ophthalmologists are on the front lines of dealing with these diseases through direct contact with patients. However, some of the most interesting careers in eye care are behind the scenes in laboratories where scientists, like modern-day explorers, investigate the origins and develop cutting-edge cures for debilitating diseases such as glaucoma, retinitis pigmentosa, and macular degeneration. These diseases were once rarely heard of. Today, it is not uncommon for well-known public figures to promote these research efforts on the television or radio. Although a great deal of progress is being made, too many Americans still lose their sight to eye diseases caused by birth defects, infections, aging, injuries, and other causes that cannot be corrected with glasses or surgery.

Here is a brief description of the major eye diseases:

## Cataracts

A cataract is the clouding of the normally transparent lens that is associated with advancing age, but it can be caused by other factors. One in every six people over the age of forty has a cataract. More than one million cataract operations are performed each year. Most are combined with the implanting of an artificial lens and can be done as same-day surgery without complications.

Recent studies show that exposure to UV light (sunlight) may contribute to the development of cataracts, and that by wearing the proper sunglasses and a wide-brimmed hat, you may protect your eyes from the early onset of this condition. However, by the age of eighty, half of all Americans have developed a cataract. Fortunately, cataract surgery is the most frequently performed operation in the United States, and it is considered a safe procedure with most costs covered by Medicare. In the rest of the world where cataract surgery is less accessible, this disease is the leading cause of blindness.

## Glaucoma

Although glaucoma is considered the most preventable form of blindness, it still claims the vision of almost eighty thousand Americans a year. It is often called a "sneak thief," because by the time you discover that you have glaucoma, it has already damaged your vision. It is estimated that probably one million people are at risk for losing their vision because they have no symptoms and have not had the comprehensive eye examination that would detect the disease. African Americans are at high risk because of the inherited form of glaucoma that has become the most prevalent cause of blindness among members of this population. Glaucoma is actually a group of diseases in which the patient experiences a loss of visual field due to damage to the optic nerve caused by increasing intraocular pressure (IOP). Open-angle glaucoma is the most common form of the disease, in which fluid is blocked in the front section of the eye causing damage to the optic nerve. The onset of angle-closure glaucoma, which is caused by pressure building between the iris and cornea, can be chronic (the IOP increases slowly and persistently) or acute (the IOP increases suddenly). Both open-angle and angle-closure glaucoma can be primary (attributed to a known cause such as inherited disease) or secondary (caused by a previous injury or illness). People who suffer from the little-understood normal or low-tension glaucoma sustain damage to the optic nerve even though their IOP is within normal ranges. Childhood or congenital glaucoma affects infants, young children, and adolescents. Fortunately, if detected early, treatment is available in the form of oral medications or eye drops that lower the IOP and surgery that uses either lasers or ophthalmic surgical instruments.

## Diabetic Retinopathy

In the United States, there are more than five million people with diagnosed diabetic retinopathy. This disease, which causes deterioration, leaking, blockages, and overgrowth of the retinal blood vessels, affects about half of all diabetics. The length of time that one has diabetes affects the occurrence of the retinopathy, making those who have experienced the juvenile-onset of the disease most at risk for vision problems. The best way to prevent diabetic retinopathy is to monitor for or control diabetes. If your vision is affected, there is a common outpatient surgery called focal photo-coagulation that when performed by a qualified ophthalmologist using a laser will seal a single leaking blood vessel. Another laser procedure, scatter photocoagulation, destroys multiple vessels and thus controls their abnormal growth. Vitrectomy is a procedure that is used for more severe cases that require that the blood-engorged vitreous be removed and replaced with a clear fluid.

## Age-Related Macular Degeneration (AMD)

The macula is the center of the retina. Most cases of macular degeneration are of the "dry" type, in which the sensitive tissues of the macula slowly become thinner and atrophy, causing a dimming of vision. There is some recent research that suggests that a diet rich in antioxidants can slow the aging process, including the progression of macular degeneration. For the rarer forms of "wet" macular degeneration, which is characterized by hemorrhaging in the retina, laser surgery can be helpful in destroying the abnormal blood vessels that cause a blind spot in the visual field. Macular degeneration is the leading cause of blindness in people over the age of fifty-five, but it can occur in young people, too. Research on this condition is proceeding aggressively. There is no effective treatment for dry AMD at the current time.

## Strabismus, Amblyopia, and Ptosis

These diseases affect at least 2 to 4 percent of children. Strabismus is the misalignment of the two eyes. It is sometimes present at birth or can occur later in life as a paralysis of the muscles that control the position of the eye. Treatment includes corrective lenses and sometimes surgery. Amblyopia, also known as "lazy eye," is a misfocus of one or both eyes that prevents normal development of vision. Treatment can include placing a patch over the stronger eye to retrain the amblyopic one.

Ptosis is a condition that causes the upper eyelid to droop and may cause amblyopia in both children and adults. Surgery to tighten the levators, or eyelid-lifting muscles, is usually the only solution to this problem.

## AIDS and the Eye

Most people know that Acquired Immunodeficiency Syndrome (AIDS) is transmitted through transfusions of infected blood. But can you get AIDS through contact with tears? No cases of AIDS have ever been attributed to contact with tears, even though the HIV virus can be found in the tears of infected persons. For people with AIDS, regular eye examinations are of critical importance. There are several complications of the disease that affect vision, including white spots or "cotton wool spots" on the retina; red eyes; detached retina; and Kaposi's sarcoma of the eyelid or white of the eye. Fortunately, ophthalmologists have several medications that eliminate or stabilize these conditions.

# Appendix A

# *Professional Organizations*

THE ORGANIZATIONS LISTED here are the major professional associations for the occupations discussed in this book. A look at their websites and publications will give you information about the latest developments in the profession, as well as an idea of the issues and concerns of this group. Other eye care organizations are listed in Appendix B.

## U.S. Organizations

American Academy of Ophthalmology
P.O. Box 7424
San Francisco, CA 94120-7424
(415) 561-8500
eyenet.org

American Association of Colleges of Osteopathic Medicine
(AACOM)
5550 Friendship Blvd.
Chevy Chase, MD 20815
aacom.org

American Optometric Association
243 N. Lindbergh Blvd.
St. Louis, MO 63141-7881
(314) 991-4000
aoanet.org

American Osteopathic College of Ophthalmology and
Otolaryngology—Head and Neck Surgery (AOCOO-HNS)
405 W. Grand Ave.
Dayton, OH 45405
(800) 455-9404
aocoohns.org

American Society of Ophthalmic Administrators
4000 Legato Rd., Ste. 850
Fairfax, VA 22033
(703) 591-2220
asoa.org

American Society of Ophthalmic Registered Nurses (ASORN)
P.O. Box 193030
San Francisco, CA 94119
(415) 561-8513
asorn.org

Association of American Medical Colleges (AAMC)
2450 N St. NW
Washington, DC 20037-1126
(202) 828-0400
aamc.org

The Association for Research in Vision and Ophthalmology
   (ARVO)
12300 Twinbrook Pkwy., Ste. 250
Rockville, MD 20852-1606
(240) 221-2900
arvo.org

Association of Schools and Colleges of Optometry (ASCO)
6110 Executive Blvd., Ste. 510
Rockville, MD 20852
(301) 231-5944
opted.org

Association of Technical Personnel in Ophthalmology
2025 Woodlane Dr.
St. Paul, MN 55125-2995
(800) 482-4858
atpo.org

Association for Vision Sciences Librarians (AVSL)
spectacle.berkeley.edu/~library/avsl.htm

National Academy of Opticianry (NAO)
8401 Corporate Dr., #605
Landover, MD 20785
(800) 229-4828

Ophthalmic Photographers Society (OPS)
213 Lorene
Nixa, MO 65714
(800) 403-1677
webeye.ophth.uiowas.edu/ops

# Canadian Organizations

Canadian Association of Optometrists
234 Argyle Ave.
Ottawa, ON K2P 1B9
(613) 235-7924
opto.ca

Canadian Ophthalmological Society
1512 Carling Ave., Ste. 610
Ottawa, ON K1Z 8R9
(800) 267-5763
eyesite.ca

Opticians Association of Canada
214-160 Hargrave St.
Winnipeg, MN R3C 3H3
(800) 847-3155
opticians.ca

# Publications and Websites

FOLLOWING ARE SOME publications and websites that will provide a variety of information for anyone interested in eye care careers.

## Publications

Green, Marianne. *Internship Success*. Lincolnwood, IL: VGM Career Books, 1998.

Kisanne, Sharon F. *Career Success for People with Physical Disabilities*. Lincolnwood, IL: VGM Career Books, 1997.

Kramer, Marc. *Power Networking: Using the Contacts You Don't Even Know You Have to Get the Job You Want*. Lincolnwood, IL: VGM Career Books, 1997.

Paradis, Adrian A. *Opportunities in Part-Time and Summer Jobs*. Lincolnwood, IL: VGM Career Books, 1997.

*Résumés for Health and Medical Careers*. Lincolnwood, IL: VGM Career Books, 1997.

*Résumés for Science Careers*. Lincolnwood, IL: VGM Career Books, 1997.

Riley, Margaret, and Frances Roehm. *The Guide to Internet Job Searching.* Chicago: VGM Career Books, 2002.
Rogers, Carla. *How to Get into the Right Medical School.* Lincolnwood, IL: VGM Career Books, 1996.

# Websites

Websites change, so it is important to know how to use an Internet search engine to find current information. One of the most popular search engines is Google (google.com). Whichever site you choose, learn the searching techniques for your system and remember that when you are searching you must think of all of the forms of a word and its synonyms to do a comprehensive job. For instance, when you are looking for "eye care" topics, you should also search under the terms "vision," "optometric," "ophthalmic," and so forth. The websites provided here are sponsored by major organizations and should be there when you go to look at them. If not, try the home page for the sponsor. And don't forget to look at the "Links" section of a site you like for similar websites. Happy browsing!

EyeCare America

eyecareamerica.org

Sponsored by the American Academy of Ophthalmology, this site has information about volunteer opportunities and special programs offered by AAO members, including free exams for seniors. Link to the "Museum of Vision," which includes a tour of the historical collection, activities for children, and resources for teachers.

Healthy Vision 2010

healthyvision2010.org

This is the nation's plan for significantly improving the visual health of the American people by the year 2010. A description of the major problems, including statistics, and the strategies for improvement are detailed in the report. This could also serve as your blueprint for finding jobs and volunteer opportunities.

Lions Club International
lionsclubs.org

Maybe you thought that the Lions Club only recycled eyeglasses. On this site, the "Vision Programs" section describes the myriad services that the Lions Club provides to the blind and to help prevent blindness. Free screenings, corneal transplants, guide dogs, camps for visually impaired children, and special equipment in public libraries for the visually impaired are only a few of its projects. Contact your local Lions Club to try out an eye care career through volunteer work.

National Eye Institute
nei.nih.gov

This is a very interesting site with the latest information on eye research. Don't miss the "Photos, Images, and Videos" section, which has copyright-free images, eye-test charts, and a fascinating section on "eye disease simulations." You can see for yourself how your vision would be affected by various diseases. There is also a list of research jobs (fellowships) available at NEI.

ORBIS
orbis.org

This is the website for the flying eye hospital that travels throughout the world helping people who need eye care. There is a very interesting online tour of this DC-10 that is equipped as a minihospital complete with an operating room. There are also interesting stories about the staff and a posting of job openings.

Prevent Blindness America
preventblindness.org

This is an organization that aggressively fights blindness in many ways, including free screenings, community and professional education, and clinical research. The website contains easy-to-understand information about the anatomy of the eye, descriptions of diseases, an eye test that you can take online, and information about volunteer opportunities.

# Educational Programs

IN THIS APPENDIX you will find accredited programs in ophthalmology, optometry, and opticianry as well as accredited training programs for ophthalmic technicians, technologists, and medical assistants.

## Accredited Residency Programs in Ophthalmology

The following programs are accredited by the Accreditation Council for Graduate Medical Education (ACGME). For more information and online links to the programs, log on to acgme.org.

### *Alabama*

University of Alabama Medical Center
Callahan Eye Foundation Hospital
700 S. Eighteenth St., Ste. 601
Birmingham, AL 35233-0342
health.uab.edu/eyes

## *Arizona*

University of Arizona College of Medicine
P.O. Box 245085
1501 N. Campbell Ave.
Tucson, AZ 85724-5085
medicine.arizona.edu

## *Arkansas*

University of Arkansas for Medical Sciences
4301 W. Markham St., Slot 523
Little Rock, AK 72205-7199
uams.edu

## *California*

California Pacific Medical Center
Department of Ophthalmology
2340 Clay St., Fifth Fl.
San Francisco, CA 94115
cpmc.org

Loma Linda University Medical Center
11234 Anderson St., #1800
Loma Linda, CA 92354
llu.edu/llumc

Martin Luther King, Jr.—Drew Medical Center
12021 S. Wilmington Ave.
Los Angeles, CA 90059
dhs.co.la.ca.us/mlk

Naval Medical Center (San Diego)
34800 Bob Wilson Dr.
San Diego, CA 92134-5000
nmcsd.med.navy.mil

Stanford University Medical Center
Department of Ophthalmology, Rm. A 157
Stanford, CA 94305-5308
med.stanford.edu

University of California (Davis) Medical Center
4860 Y St., Ste. 2400
Sacramento, CA 95817
ucdmc.ucdavis.edu

University of California (Irvine) College of Medicine
118 Med Surge
Irvine, CA 92647
com.uci.edu

UCLA School of Medicine
100 Stein Plaza—CHS
Ste. #2-247
Los Angeles, CA 90095-7000
medsch.ucla.edu

University of California (San Diego)
UCSD Shiley Eye Center (MC0946)
9415 Campus Point Dr.
La Jolla, CA 92037-1350
http://eyesite.ucsd.edu

University of California (San Francisco) School of Medicine
Department of Ophthalmology, K-301
10 Koret Way
San Francisco, CA 94143-0730
som.ucsf.edu/som

University of Southern California Medical Center
Doheny Eye Center
1450 San Pablo St.
Los Angeles, CA 90033
usc.edu/hsc/doheny

## Colorado

University of Colorado Health Sciences Center
P.O. Box 6510
Mail Stop F731
Aurora, CO 80045
uchsc.edu

## Connecticut

Yale University School of Medicine
330 Cedar St.
P.O. Box 208061
New Haven, CT 06520-8061
http://info.med.yale.edu/ysm

## District of Columbia

George Washington University
2150 Pennsylvania Ave. NW, Fl. 2A
Washington, DC 20037
gwu.edu

Georgetown University Hospital/Washington Hospital Center
110 Irving St. NW, Ste. 1A-1
Washington, DC 20010
whcenter.org

Georgetown University Medical Center
3800 Reservoir Rd. NW (7PHC)
Washington, DC 20007-2197
http://gumc.georgetown.edu

Howard University Hospital
2041 Georgia Ave. NW, Ste. 2100
Washington, DC 20060
huhosp.org

Walter Reed Army Medical Center
Ophthalmology Service, Department of Surgery
6900 Georgia Ave. NW
Washington, DC 20307
wramc.amedd.army.mil

## *Florida*

University of Florida Health Science Center
Department of Ophthalmology
Box 100284 JHMHC
Gainesville, FL 32610-6284
health.ufl.edu

University of South Florida College of Medicine
MDC—Box 21
12901 Bruce B. Downs Blvd.
Tampa, FL 33612-4766
http://hsc.usf.edu/med.html

## *Georgia*

Emory University School of Medicine
Emory Eye Center, Ste. B 2400
1365 B Clifton Rd. NE
Atlanta, GA 30322-4766
emory.edu/whsc/med

Medical College of Georgia School of Medicine
1120 Fifteenth St.
Augusta, GA 30912-3400
mcg.edu/som/index.html

## *Illinois*

Cook County Hospital
Division of Ophthalmology
1835 W. Harrison St.
Chicago, IL 60612-9985
cchil.org

Loyola University, Stritch School of Medicine
Foster G. McGaw Hospital
2160 S. First Ave.
Maywood, IL 60153
meddean.luc.edu

McGaw Medical Center of Northwestern University
645 N. Michigan Ave., Ste. 440
Chicago, IL 60611-3833
http://feinberg.northwestern.edu/clinical_services/mcgaw.htm

Rush Presbyterian–St. Luke's Medical Center
1653 W. Congress Pkwy.
Chicago, IL 60612-3864
rush.edu

University of Chicago Hospital and Clinics
Department of Ophthalmology and Visual Science
Visual Sciences Center
5841 S. Maryland Ave., MC 2114
Chicago, IL 60637-1470
http://uchospitals.edu

University of Illinois Eye and Ear Infirmary
Ophthalmology Education Office, Rm. 159
1855 W. Taylor St.
Chicago, IL 60612
http://uic.edu/com/eye

## *Indiana*

Indiana University Hospitals
Department of Ophthalmology
702 Rotary Circle
Indianapolis, IN 46202-5175
http://medicine.iu.edu

## *Iowa*

University of Iowa Hospitals and Clinics
Department of Ophthalmology
200 Hawkins Dr.
Iowa City, IA 52242-1009
uihealthcare.com/uihospitalsandclinics

## Kansas

University of Kansas Medical Center
3901 and Rainbow Blvd.
2003 Sudler
Kansas City, KS 66160-7379
kumc.edu

## Kentucky

University of Kentucky—Chandler Medical Center
Department of Ophthalmology
E 304 Kentucky Clinic
Lexington, KY 40536-0284
mc.uky.edu

University of Louisville
Department of Ophthalmology
301 E. Muhammad Ali Blvd.
Kentucky Lions Eye Center
Louisville, KY 40202
louisville.edu/medschool/ophthalmology

## Louisiana

Louisiana State University Health Sciences Center
Department of Ophthalmology
LSU Eye Center
2020 Gravier St., Ste. B
New Orleans, LA 70112-2234
lsumc.edu

Louisiana State University Hospital (Shreveport)
P.O. Box 33932
1501 Kings Highway
Shreveport, LA 71130-3932
sh.lsuhsc.edu

Tulane University School of Medicine
1430 Tulane Ave.
New Orleans, LA 70112-2699
tulane.edu/academics_sch_med.cfm

## *Maryland*

Johns Hopkins University Medical Center
Wilmer Institute, B20
600 N. Wolfe St.
Baltimore, MD 21287-9121
wilmer.jhu.edu/departments/baymed.htm

Maryland General Hospital
827 Linden Ave.
Baltimore, MD 21201
marylandgeneral.org

University of Maryland Medical Center
Department of Ophthalmology
22 S. Green St.
Baltimore, MD 21201-1590
umm.edu

## *Massachusetts*

Boston University Medical Center
Department of Ophthalmology
80 E. Concord St.—L907
Boston, MA 02118-2394
bumc.bu.edu/departments/homemain.asp?departmentid=74

Massachusetts Eye and Ear Infirmary
243 Charles St.
Boston, MA 02114-3094
meei.harvard.edu

## *Michigan*

Henry Ford Hospital
2799 W. Grand Blvd., K-10
Detroit, MI 48202-2689
henryford.com

University of Michigan Medical School
W. K. Kellogg Eye Center
Box 0714, 1000 Wall St.
Ann Arbor, MI 48105-1912
med.umich.edu/medschool

Wayne State University
Kresge Eye Institute
4717 St. Antoine
Detroit, MI 48201-1423
med.wayne.edu/kresgeeye

William Beaumont Hospital
3601 W. Thirteen Mile Rd.
Royal Oak, MI 48073
beaumonthospitals.com

## *Minnesota*

Mayo Graduate School of Medicine
Department of Ophthalmology
200 First St. SW
Rochester, MN 55905
mayo.edu/mgs

University of Minnesota
Department of Ophthalmology
MMC 493, 420 Delaware St. SE
Minneapolis, MN 55455-0501
med.umn.edu/ophthalmology

## *Mississippi*

University of Mississippi Medical Center
2500 N. State St.
McBryde Bldg., Third Fl.
Jackson, MS 39216
umc.edu

## *Missouri*

St. Louis University School of Medicine
Anheuser Busch Eye Institute
1755 S. Grand Blvd.
St. Louis, MO 63104-4505
sluei.slu.edu

University of Missouri—Columbia Hospital and Clinics
One Hospital Dr.
Mason Institute of Ophthalmology
Columbia, MO 65212
muhealth.org

University of Missouri at Kansas City
School of Medicine
2300 Homes St.
Kansas City, MO 64108
http://research.med.umkc.edu

Washington University School of Medicine
660 S. Euclid Campus, Box 8096
St. Louis, MO 63110
http://medicine.wustl.edu

## *Nebraska*

University of Nebraska Medical Center
600 S. Forty-Second St.
Omaha, NE 68198-5540
unmc.edu

## *New Jersey*

University of Medicine and Dentistry of New Jersey (UMDNJ)
New Jersey Medical School
Department of Ophthalmology
90 Bergen St., DOC-Sixth Fl.
Newark, NJ 07103-2499
http://njms.umdnj.edu

University of Medicine and Dentistry of New Jersey (UMDNJ)
Robert Wood Johnson Medical School
675 Hoes La.
Piscataway, NJ 08854
http://rwjms.umdnj.edu

## *New York*

Albany Medical Center
Lions Eye Center
35 Hackett Blvd.
Albany, NY 12208-2499
amc.edu/patient/lions/lions.htm

Albert Einstein College of Medicine
Montefiore Medical Center
East 210th St. and Bainbridge Ave.
Bronx, NY 10467-2490
montefiore.org

Albert Einstein College of Medicine
Long Island Jewish Medical Center
Department of Ophthalmology
600 Northern Blvd., Ste. 214
Great Neck, NY 10021-2490
lij.edu/lijh/ophthalmology/ophthalmology.html

Bronx-Lebanon Hospital Center
1650 Selwyn Ave., 10G
Bronx, NY 10457
bronx-leb.org

Interfaith Medical Center
Department of Ophthalmology
528 Prospect Pl.
Brooklyn, NY 11238
interfaithmedical.com

Mount Sinai School of Medicine
Department of Ophthalmology
1 Gustave L. Levy Place, Box 1183
New York, NY 10029-6574
mssm.edu

Nassau University Medical Center
2201 Hempstead Turnpike
East Meadow, NY 11554-4297
numc.edu

New York Eye and Ear Infirmary
310 E. Fourteenth St.
New York, NY 10003-4297
nyee.edu

New York Medical College
St. Vincent Catholic Medical Centers (Brooklyn and Queens)
88-25 153rd St., 4-H
Jamaica, NY 11432
svcmc.org/portal/default.asp

New York Medical College (Manhattan)
St. Vincent's Catholic Medical Centers
170 W. Twelfth St.
New York, NY 10011-8305
svcmc.org/portal/default.asp

New York Medical College
Westchester County Medical Center
Department of Ophthalmology
Valhalla, NY 10595
nymc.edu

New York and Presbyterian Hospital (Columbia Campus)
635 W. 165th St.
New York, NY 10032-2499
nyp.org

New York and Presbyterian Hospital (Cornell Campus)
525 E. Sixty-Eighth St., Rm. K-811
New York, NY 10021-2098
nyp.org

New York University Medical Center
550 First Ave.
NBV 5N 18
New York, NY 10016
med.nyu.edu

NYU School of Medicine
North Shore University Hospital
600 Northern Blvd., Ste. 220
Great Neck, NY 11021
med.nyu.edu

St. Luke's–Roosevelt Hospital Center
1111 Amsterdam Ave.
Ophthalmology Department
New York, NY 10025
wehealny.org/patients/slr_description.html

SUNY Health Science Center (Brooklyn)
450 Clarkson Ave., SUNY-HSCB
Department of Ophthalmology
Brooklyn, NY 11203-2098
hscbklyn.edu
sunybklynem.org

SUNY at Buffalo
Children's Hospital
Department of Ophthalmology
219 Bryant St.
Buffalo, NY 14222
chob.edu/clinical_services/ophthalmology.html
http://wings.buffalo.edu/smbs

SUNY Upstate Medical University
550 Harrison St., Ste. 340
Syracuse, NY 13202
upstate.edu

University of Rochester Medical Center
P.O. Box 659
601 Elmwood Ave.
Rochester, NY 14642
urmc.rochester.edu

## North Carolina

Duke University Medical Center
Duke Eye Center, DUMC 3802
Erwin Rd.
Durham, NC 27710
mc.duke.edu

University of North Carolina Hospitals
Department of Ophthalmology
617 Burnett Womack Bldg., CB7040
Chapel Hill, NC 27599-7040
med.unc.edu

Wake Forest University School of Medicine
Department of Ophthalmology
Medical Center Blvd.
Winston-Salem, NC 27157-1033
wfubmc.edu/school

## Ohio

Case Western Reserve/University Hospitals of Cleveland
11100 Euclid Ave.
Cleveland, OH 44106-5068
uhhs.com

Cleveland Clinic Foundation
Cole Eye Institute, Desk I-32
9500 Euclid Ave.
Cleveland, OH 44195
clevelandclinic.org

Ohio State University Hospital Clinic
5251 Henry G. Cramblett Hall
456 W. Tenth Ave.
Columbus, OH 43210-1228
osumedcenter.edu

Summa Health System
41 Arch St., Ste. 219
Akron, OH 44304
summahealth.org

University of Cincinnati Medical Center
Department of Ophthalmology
Eden Ave. and Albert Sabin Way (ML 527)
Cincinnati, OH 45267-0527
http://medcenter.uc.edu

## Oklahoma

University of Oklahoma Medical Center
Dean A. McGee Eye Institute
608 Stanton L. Young Dr.
Oklahoma City, OK 73104
dmei.org

## *Oregon*

Oregon Health and Sciences University
Casey Eye Institute
3,75 Terwilliger Blvd.
Portland, OR 97201-4197
ohsuhealth.com/cei

## *Pennsylvania*

Drexel University College of Medicine (MCP/Hahnemann) System
219 N. Broad St., Third Fl.
Mail Stop 209
Philadelphia, PA 19107
drexel.edu/med

Geisinger Medical Center
Department of Ophthalmology
North Academy Dr.
Danville, PA 17822-2120
geisinger.org/about/gmc.shtml

Pennsylvania State University/Milton S. Hershey Medical Center
P.O. Box 850, MC HU19
500 University Dr.
Hershey, PA 17033-0850
hmc.psu.edu

Temple University School of Medicine
Department of Ophthalmology
3401 N. Broad St.
Philadelphia, PA 19140
medschool.temple.edu

University Health Center of Pittsburgh
Eye and Ear Institute of Pittsburgh
203 Lothrop St.
Pittsburgh, PA 15213
upmc.edu/eyeear

University of Pennsylvania Health System
Scheie Eye Institute
Myrin Circle, 51 N. Thirty-Ninth St.
Philadelphia, PA 19104
penneye.com/html/scheie_eye_institute.html

Wills Eye Hospital
Ninth and Walnut Sts.
Philadelphia, PA 19107-5598
willseye.org/default.htm

## Puerto Rico

University of Puerto Rico
Medical Sciences Campus
P.O. Box 365067
San Juan, PR 00936-5067
upr.clu.edu

## Rhode Island

Brown University/Rhode Island Hospital
593 Eddy St., APC-712
Providence, RI 02903
lifespan.org/partners/rih
http://biomed.brown.edu/medicine/hospitals/
    affiliated_hospitals.html

## *South Carolina*

Medical University of South Carolina
Storm Eye Institute
167 Ashely Ave., P.O. Box 250676
Charleston, SC 29425-2236
stormeye.musc.edu

Richland Memorial Hospital
University of South Carolina School of Medicine
4 Richland Medical Park, Ste. 300
Columbia, SC 29203
med.sc.edu

## *Tennessee*

Chattanooga Unit—University of Tennessee College of Medicine
Department of Ophthalmology
975 E. Third St.
Chattanooga, TN 37403
utcomchatt.org

The University of Tennessee (Memphis)
Department of Ophthalmology
956 Court Ave., Ste. D228
Memphis, TN 38163
utmem.edu

Vanderbilt University School of Medicine
Vanderbilt Eye Institute
1215 Twenty-First Ave. E.
Eighth Fl., Vanderbilt MC E.
Nashville, TN 37232-8808
mc.vanderbilt.edu/vumcdept/ophthal

## *Texas*

Baylor College of Medicine
Department of Ophthalmology
6565 Fannin, NC205
Houston, TX 77030-9057
bcm.tmc.edu

San Antonio Uniformed Services Health Education Consortium
Wilford Hall Medical Center/MCST
2200 Bergquist Dr.
Lackland AFB, TX 78236-5300
whmc.af.mil

Texas A&M College of Medicine
Scott and White Graduate Memorial Hall
2401 S. Thirty-First St.
Temple, TX 76508-3900
http://medicine.tamu.edu

Texas Tech University (Lubbock)
Department of Ophthalmology/Visual Science
3601 Fourth St.
Lubbock, TX 79430
remedy.ttuhsc.edu/eye

University of Texas
Southwestern Medical School
5323 Harry Hines Blvd.
Dallas, TX 75235-9057
swmed.edu

University of Texas Medical Branch at Galveston
Department of Ophthalmology
700 University Blvd.
Galveston, TX 77555
utmb.edu

University of Texas at Houston
Department of Ophthalmology
6431 Fannin, MSB7.024
Houston, TX 77030
med.uth.tmc.edu

University of Texas Health Science Center at San Antonio
Department of Ophthalmology
7703 Floyd Curl Dr., Mail Code 6230
San Antonio, TX 78229-3900
uthscsa.edu

## Utah

University of Utah Health Sciences Center
John A. Moran Eye Center
50 N. Medical Dr.
Salt Lake City, UT 84132
http://insight.med.utah.edu

## Virginia

Eastern Virginia Medical School
Department of Ophthalmology
880 Kempsville Rd., Ste. 2500
Norfolk, VA 23502-3990
evms.edu

University of Virginia Health System
P.O. Box 800715
Charlottesville, VA 22908-0715
http://hsc.virginia.edu

Virginia Commonwealth University Health System
Medical College of Virginia Hospital
1101 E. Marshall St.
P.O. Box 980262
Richmond, VA 23298-0262
vcuhealth.org

## Washington

Madigan Army Medical Center
Attn: MCHJ-SOU
Ophthalmology Service
Tacoma, WA 98431
mamc.amedd.army.mil/wrmc/wrmcfront.asp

University of Washington School of Medicine
Department of Ophthalmology, Box 356485
1959 NE Pacific
Seattle, WA 98195-6485
washington.edu/medical/som

## West Virginia

West Virginia University School of Medicine
WVU Eye Institute, Department of Ophthalmology
P.O. Box 9193, Stadium Dr.
Morgantown, WV 26506
hsc.wvu.edu/som/eye

## *Wisconsin*

Medical College of Wisconsin
The Eye Institute
925 N. Eighty-Seventh St.
Milwaukee, WI 53226
mcw.edu

University of Wisconsin Medical Center
F4/336 Clinical Science Center
600 Highland Ave.
Madison, WI 53792
med.wisc.edu

# Schools of Optometry

The following programs are accredited by the American Optometric Association (AOA). For more information log on to opted.org.

## *Alabama*

University of Alabama School of Optometry
The Medical Center
1716 University Blvd.
Birmingham, AL 35294-0010
http://ntopt.opt.uab.edu/icare

## *California*

Southern California College of Optometry
2575 Yorba Linda Blvd.
Fullerton, CA 92831
scco.edu

University of California (Berkeley)
School of Optometry
390 Minor Hall
Berkeley, CA 94720-2020
http://spectacle.berkeley.edu

## *Florida*

NOVA Southeastern University
College of Optometry
3200 S. University Dr.
Fort Lauderdale, FL 33328
nova.edu/cwis/centers/hpd/optometry

## *Illinois*

Illinois College of Optometry
3241 S. Michigan Ave.
Chicago, IL 60616
ico.edu

## *Indiana*

Indiana University
School of Optometry
800 E. Atwater Ave.
Bloomington, IN 47405
opt.indiana.edu

## *Massachusetts*

New England College of Optometry
424 Beacon St.
Boston, MA 02115
ne-optometry.edu

## *Michigan*

Michigan College of Optometry at Ferris State
1310 Cramer Circle
Big Rapids, MI 49307
ferris.edu/mco/homepage.html

## *Missouri*

University of Missouri (St. Louis)
College of Optometry
8001 Natural Bridge Rd.
St. Louis, MO 63121
umsl.edu/divisions/optometry/optometry.html

## *New York*

State University of New York
State College of Optometry
33 W. Forty-Second St.
New York, NY 10036
sunyopt.edu

## *Ohio*

Ohio State University
College of Optometry
320 W. Tenth Ave.
P.O. Box 182342
Columbus, OH 43210-2342
http://optometry.osu.edu

## *Oklahoma*

Northeastern State University
College of Optometry
1001 N. Grand Ave.
Tahlequah, OK 74464
http://arapaho.nsuok.edu/~optometry

## *Oregon*

Pacific University
College of Optometry
2043 College Way
Forest Grove, OR 97116
opt.pacificu.edu

## *Pennsylvania*

Pennsylvania College of Optometry
Elkins Park Campus
8360 Old York Rd.
Elkins Park, PA 19027
pco.edu

## *Puerto Rico*

InterAmerican University
School of Optometry
118 Eleanor Roosevelt
Hato Rey, PR 00919
optonet.inter.edu

## *Tennessee*

Southern College of Optometry
1245 Madison Ave.
Memphis, TN 38104
sco.edu

## *Texas*

University of Houston
College of Optometry
505 J. Davis Armistead Bldg.
Houston, TX 77204-2020
opt.uh.edu

# Schools of Opticianry

The following programs are members of the National Federation
of Opticianry Schools (nfos.org). Those schools followed by an
asterisk (*) have a distance learning program.

## *California*

American Career College
Optical Dispensing
4021 Rosewood Ave.
Los Angeles, CA 90004
americancareer.com/programs/optical

Palomar Community College
Optical Technology
1140 W. Mission Rd.
San Marcos, CA 92069-1487
palomar.edu

## *Colorado*

T. H. Pickens Technical Center
Opticianry
500 Airport Blvd.
Aurora, CO 80011

## *Connecticut*

Middlesex Community College
Ophthalmic Design and Dispensing
100 Training Hill Rd.
Middletown, CT 06547
mxctc.commnet.edu/mxhome/mxhome.htm

# *Florida*

Hillsborough Community College*
Ophthalmic Dispensing
P.O. Box 30030
Tampa, FL 33630-3030
hcc.cc.fl.us

Miami-Dade Community College
Vision Care Tech/Opticianry
Medical Center Campus
950 NW Twentieth St.
Miami, FL 33127
mdcc.edu

# *Georgia*

DeKalb Technical Institute*
Opticianry
495 N. Indian Creek Dr.
Clarkston, GA 30021
dekalb.tec.ga.us

Ogeechee Technical College
Opticianry
One Joe Kennedy Blvd.
Statesboro, GA 30458
ogeechee.org

## *Hawaii*

Leeward Community College
96-045 Ala Ike
Pearl City, HI 96782-3393
lcc.hawaii.edu

## *Indiana*

Indiana University
Optician/Technician Program
School of Optometry
800 E. Atwater
Bloomington, IN 47405
opt.indiana.edu/programs/opttech/opttech.htm

## *Massachusetts*

Holyoke Community College
Opticianry Program
303 Homestead Ave.
Holyoke, MA 01040
hcc.mass.edu

Quinsigamond Community College
670 Boylston St.
Worchester, MA 01606-2092
qcc.mass.edu

## *Michigan*

Ferris State University
Opticianry
200 Ferris Dr.
1310 Cramer
Big Rapids, MI 49307-2738
ferris.edu

## *Nevada*

Community College of Southern Nevada
Ophthalmic Technology/Ophthalmic Dispensing
6375 W. Charleston Blvd., W1A
Las Vegas, NV 89146-1164
ccsn.nevada.edu

## *New Jersey*

Camden County College
Opticianry
P.O. Box 200
Blackwood, NJ 08012
camdencc.edu

Essex County College
Opticianry
303 University Ave.
Newark, NJ 07102
essex.edu

Raritan Valley Community College
Ophthalmic Science
P.O. Box 3300
Somerville, NJ 08876-1265
raritanval.edu

## *New Mexico*

Southwestern Indian Polytechnic Institute
Optical Technology
9169 Coors Rd. NW
Albuquerque, NM 87184
sipi.bia.edu

## *New York*

Erie Community College
Ophthalmic Dispensing
6205 Main St.
Williamsville, NY 14221-7095
ecc.edu

Interboro Institute
Ophthalmic Dispensing
450 W. Fifty-Sixth St.
New York, NY 10019
interboro.com

New York City Technical College
Opticianry
300 Jay St.
Brooklyn, NY 11201
citytech.cuny.edu

Rochester Institute of Technology
Ophthalmic Optical Finishing Technology
52 Lomb Memorial Dr.
LBJ Bldg.
Rochester, NY 14623-0887
rit.edu/~932www/ugrad_bulletin/colleges/ntid/optical.html

Suffolk County Community College, Western Campus
Opticianry
Crooked Hill Rd.
Brentwood, NY 11717
sunysuffolk.edu

## *North Carolina*

Durham Technical Community College*
Opticianry
1637 Lawson St.
Durham, NC 27703
durhamtech.org

## *Ohio*

Owens Community College
Optometric/Ophthalmic Technology
P.O. Box 10000
Oregon Rd.
Toledo, OH 43699-1947
owens.edu

## *Tennessee*

The Learning Center
P.O. Box 5170
Sevierville, TN 37864-5170

Roane State Community College
Opticianry
Patton Lane
Harriman, TN 37748
rscc.cc.tn.us

## *Texas*

El Paso Community College
Ophthalmic Technology
P.O. Box 20500
El Paso, TX 79998
epcc.edu

Tyler Junior College
Ophthalmic Technology
1400 E. Fifth St.
Tyler, TX 75798
tyler.cc.tx.us

## *Vermont*

Community College of Vermont*
Opticianry Program
P.O. Box 120
Waterbury, VT 05676-0120
ccv.vsc.edu

## *Virginia*

J. Sargeant Reynolds Community College*
Opticianry
P.O. Box 85622
Richmond, VA 23285-5622
jsr.cc.va.us

Naval Ophthalmic Support and Training Activity
Tri-Service Optician Schools (TOPS)
Thomas Nelson Community College
NWS, P.O. Box 350
Yorktown, VA 23691-0350
http://138.143.250.101/nostra

## *Washington*

Highline Community College
Opticianry
P.O. Box 9800
2400 S. 240th St.
Des Moines, WA 98198-9800
highline.ctc.edu

Seattle Central Community College
Opticianry
1701 Broadway
Seattle, WA 98122
seattlecentral.org

# Training Programs for Ophthalmic Technicians and Technologists

The following programs are accredited by the Joint Commission on Allied Health Personnel in Ophthalmology (JCAHPO).

## Colorado

Pima Medical Institute
Ophthalmic Medical Technician
1701 W. Seventy-Second St.
Denver, CO 80221
pimamedical.com

Pueblo Community College
Ophthalmic Technician
900 W. Orman Ave.
Pueblo, CO 81004
pcc.cccoes.edu

## District of Columbia

Georgetown University Medical Center
Ophthalmic Medical Personnel Training Program
3800 Reservoir Rd. NW
Washington, DC 20007
georgetown.edu/departments/ophthalmology/tech.htm

## *Florida*

University of Florida
Ophthalmic Technology Training Program
Department of Ophthalmology
P.O. Box 100284
Gainesville, FL 32610
eye.ufl.edu/optkprog.htm

## *Georgia*

Emory University
Master of Medical Science in Ophthalmic Technology
1365-B Clifton Rd. B4629
Atlanta, GA 30322
emory.edu/eye_center/research_and_education/education/master_de
    gree_frame.html

## *Illinois*

Triton College
Ophthalmic Technician Program
2000 N. Fifth Ave.
River Grove, IL 61071
triton.cc.il.us

## *Louisiana*

Louisiana State University Medical Center
Ophthalmic Medical Technology Program
2020 Gravier St., Ste. B
New Orleans, LA 70112
lsuhsc.edu/no

## *Michigan*

Detroit Institute of Ophthalmology
Ophthalmic Technology Program
15415 E. Jefferson Ave.
Grosse Pointe Park, MI 48230
brophy.com/dio

## *Minnesota*

Regions Hospital
School of Ophthalmic Medical Technology
640 Jackson St.
St. Paul, MN 55101
cce.umn.edu/certificates/opthalmic_tech.shtml

## *North Carolina*

Duke University School of Medicine
Ophthalmic Medical Technicians
Box 3802
Durham, NC 27710
dukeeye.org/education/technician.html

## *Ohio*

Lakeland Community College
Ophthalmic Technology
7700 Clocktower Dr.
Kirkland, OH 44094
lakeland.cc.oh.us

## *Oregon*

Portland Community College
Ophthalmic Medical Technology Program
Cascade Campus
P.O. Box 97280
Portland, OR 97280
pcc.edu

## *Virginia*

Old Dominion University/Eastern Medical School
Ophthalmic Technology Program
Lions Center for Sight
600 Gresham Dr.
Norfolk, VA 23507
odu.edu/ao/admissions/mp/majors/ophthalmictechnology.html

# Training Programs (Short Courses) for Ophthalmic Medical Assistants

The following programs are accredited by the Joint Commission on Allied Health Personnel in Ophthalmology (JCAHPO).

## *Arizona*

Pima Medical Institute
Ophthalmic Medical Assistant Program
3350 E. Grant Rd.
Tucson, AZ 85716
pimamedical.com

## *California*

Jules Stein Eye Institute
Ophthalmic Assistant Training
100 Stein Plaza, Rm. 3-223
Los Angeles, CA 90095
jsei.org

Naval School of Health Sciences
Ocular Technician Program
NEC 8445
San Diego, CA 92134
http://shs.med.navy.mil

## *District of Columbia*

Georgetown University Medical Center
Ophthalmic Medical Assisting Program
3800 Reservoir Rd. NW
Washington, DC 20007
georgetown.edu/departments/ophthalmology/tech.htm

## *Louisiana*

Delgado Community College
Ophthalmic Medical Assisting Program
Allied Health Division
615 City Park Ave.
New Orleans, LA 70119-4399
dcc.edu

## *Massachusetts*

Holyoke Community College
Ophthalmic Assistant Program
303 Homestead Ave.
Holyoke, MA 01040
hcc.mass.edu

## *Michigan*

Detroit Institute of Ophthalmology
Ophthalmic Assistant Program
15415 E. Jefferson Ave.
Grosse Pointe Park, MI 48230
brophy.com/dio

## *New Jersey*

Ocean County College
Ophthalmic Medical Assisting
College Dr.
Toms River, NJ 08754-2001
ocean.cc.nj.us

UMD-New Jersey
Ophthalmic Allied Health Programs
Department of Ophthalmology, Rm. 6157
90 Bergen St.
Newark, NJ 07103-2499
umdnj.edu

## *New York*

Caldwell Community College
Ophthalmic Medical Assisting
2855 Hickory Blvd.
Hudson, NY 28638

Continuing Medical Education for Ophthalmic Assistants
Ophthalmic Assistant Training Program
46 W. Eighty-Sixth St.
New York, NY 10024
cmeoa.org

## *Ohio*

Stark State College of Technology
Ophthalmic Medical Assistant Program
6200 Frank Ave. NW
Canton, OH 44720
stark.cc.oh.us

## *Texas*

Tyler Junior College
Vision Care Technology
P.O. Box 9020
Tyler, TX 75711-9020
tyler.cc.tx.us

U.S. Army Medical Department Center and Schools
300-P3 Eye Specialist Course
Department of Medical Science
2751 McIndoe Rd.
Fort Sam Houston, TX 78234
cs.amedd.army.mil

## *Washington*

Pima Medical Institute (Seattle)
Ophthalmic Medical Assistant Program
1627 Eastlake Ave. E.
Seattle, WA 98102
pimamedical.com

## *West Virginia*

West Virginia University
Ophthalmic Medical Assistant Program
Department of Ophthalmology
P.O. Box 9193
Morgantown, WV 26506-9193
hsc.wvu.edu/som/eye

# About the Author

Kathleen Belikoff personifies the idea that career opportunities abound for people who are willing to work their way up. Her own career in health care began when she took a temporary job as a medical records file clerk. She became a hospital administrator at Presbyterian Medical Center in Philadelphia and is now a health care consultant.

Ms. Belikoff grew up in suburban Baltimore and began her writing career as editor-in-chief of the Hereford High School student newspaper. She honed her writing skills as an English major at Hood College and pursued a graduate degree in education and information science at Towson State University. Her most recent publications are about her observations on the changing health care scene, including a chapter in *Using Hospital Space Profitably*, which is about converting unused hospital space into restaurants, research labs, and other revenue-producing facilities.

Her interest in writing about eye care career opportunities emanates from her association with the world-renowned Scheie Eye

Institute, which serves as the department of ophthalmology for both Presbyterian and the University of Pennsylvania Hospitals. Starting as the hospital librarian and later as an administrator, she worked with all levels of clinical staff, researchers, administrators, medical and nursing students, and patients. Today, she continues to write about health careers and works with graduate students in nursing, computer science, business, and education as a reference librarian at the Bucks County Campus of La Salle University.